The 12-Week
Journey to
Lifelong Wellness

GREGORY L. JANTZ, PhD
WITH KEITH WALL

Healing
Depression
for Life
WORKBOOK

TYNDALE
MOMENTUM®

*The nonfiction imprint of
Tyndale House Publishers, Inc.*

Visit Tyndale online at www.tyndale.com.

Visit Tyndale Momentum online at www.tyndalemomentum.com.

TYNDALE, Tyndale Momentum, and Tyndale's quill logo are registered trademarks of Tyndale House Publishers, Inc. The Tyndale Momentum logo is a trademark of Tyndale House Publishers, Inc. Tyndale Momentum is the nonfiction imprint of Tyndale House Publishers, Inc., Carol Stream, Illinois.

Healing Depression for Life Workbook: The 12-Week Journey to Lifelong Wellness

Designed by Jennifer Phelps

Edited by Jonathan Schindler

Published in association with The Bindery Agency, www.TheBinderyAgency.com.

For information about special discounts for bulk purchases, please contact Tyndale House Publishers at csresponse@tyndale.com, or call 1-800-323-9400.

ISBN 978-1-4964-3769-3

Printed in the United States of America

25	24	23	22	21	20	19
7	6	5	4	3	2	1

Contents

Building Your Success Plan

The good life is waiting for you. Right now. Right here.

Deep-down contentment and genuine happiness are available to you. Not someday, but soon.

It's fully possible to find healing for your depression. For life.

Even in our furiously fast-paced and worrisome world, you can live a more peaceful, purposeful, and productive life. You can be free from thoughts, feelings, and habits that drag you down rather than lift you up. You can learn to draw the life-numbing poison out of your past pain, present problems, and future fear.

This "good life" doesn't lie at some distant destination or at the end of year after year of seeking. It is yours for the taking—starting now. The only cost of admission is your willingness to change the way you see yourself and the world around you . . . and to consistently incorporate the healthy habits that will bring lasting wholeness. The payoff—a life infused with beauty, joy, and meaning—is well worth the investment.

I am not giving you a pep talk or offering snappy slogans to help you feel better temporarily. The last thing you need is advice that rings hollow or bromides that promise much and deliver little.

If you've been battling depression for any length of time, you have likely heard all kinds of recommendations that didn't bring you much improvement. Worse, you've probably heard plenty of clichés from well-meaning (but unhelpful) people: "Hang in there—this too shall pass" or "Keep looking up" or "Hold on to your faith."

I know that overcoming depression takes patience, dogged determination, the courage to confront painful issues, openness to new ideas, and a commitment to change long-standing patterns of behavior.

Another essential element is needed to heal depression: hope.

In three decades as a mental health expert, I have counseled thousands of people who needed help coping with pain and fear of every kind: depression, guilt, anger, anxiety, addiction, and the emotional scars of physical and psychological abuse. Early in my career, I was often dismayed by the epic scope of battles people waged within themselves and the elusive struggle to achieve true healing. It seemed to me that lasting wellness was a treasure many seek but few ever find.

Then I realized something vitally important. Many of the hurting people I counseled were eager—or desperate—to overcome their troubles but lacked the key ingredient of hope. By the time these people began therapy with me or sought treatment at the clinic I direct, they had lived with their condition for so long and tried so many unfruitful treatment options that optimism had all but vanished. Distress and depression, usually caused by a variety of factors, were compounded by a fundamental lack of hopefulness and confidence that anything would ever change.

This led me to make *hope* a cornerstone of all the therapy, speaking, writing, research, and treatment planning I do. In 1996, we changed the name of our Seattle-area treatment facility after clients said, "This is a place of hope." That's exactly what we wanted it to be, and the name stuck. Our facility is now called The Center: A Place of

Hope. My team and I also adopted Jeremiah 29:11-14 as our clinic's guiding Scripture passage:

> "I know the plans I have for you," declares the LORD, "plans to prosper you and not to harm you, plans to give you hope and a future. Then you will call on me and come and pray to me, and I will listen to you. You will seek me and find me when you seek me with all your heart. I will be found by you," declares the LORD, "and will bring you back from captivity."

I encourage you to reflect on these life-changing words and embrace them as your touchstone as you pursue emotional, spiritual, and physical wellness. After all, depressed people often feel that they are in "captivity" of sorts—trapped and immobilized by a force bigger than themselves. But God will indeed bring you back. Depressed people often do not feel enthused about the future, if they can envision one at all. But God will help you renew your dreams and refresh your energy to achieve them.

As foundational as hope is to true healing, there are many other crucial steps to take on the journey. And these steps form the twelve weeks of exercises, assessments, and reflections in the pages ahead. In addition to the need for hope, I realized something else many years ago: most approaches to depression focus on one particular method or technique to address a complex mental health conundrum. That's what has become common for the treatment of depression these days. Care providers tend to use their favorites as singular fixes to a disorder that is never caused by one thing alone. Most frequently, this means taking antidepressant medication, seeing a counselor for talk therapy, starting a specialized diet regimen, or participating in cognitive behavioral therapy.

While each of these individual approaches can be helpful and sometimes needed, I believe that lasting healing occurs through a whole-person, multifaceted approach. In my experience, depression always arises from multiple factors converging from lots of different directions in a person's life. Treating one thing at a time, with one method at a time, may move you toward healing but will usually fall short of complete healing. This is why my whole-person approach addresses the following:

- achieving ample, restorative sleep
- examining the use of technology and making sure it is not contributing to depression
- minimizing and managing stress
- uncovering hidden addictions
- resolving the three deadly emotions: anger, guilt, and fear
- working through the process of forgiveness for hurts and heartaches
- engaging in soul care and spiritual practices
- participating in consistent physical activity
- fortifying your nutrition and hydration
- detoxing your body of contaminants
- refreshing your dreams and plans for the future

These topics (along with gut health and micronutrients) are discussed in detail in *Healing Depression for Life*, where I present an array of scientific research studies, psychological principles, spiritual insights, real-life stories, and practical applications. With this companion workbook, I am handing the baton to you. It's your turn to dive in and dig deep into the *reasons* and the *remedies* for your depression. Think of me as your guide through this process—your Sherpa as you climb the mountain and move steadily toward the summit. I will point you in the right direction and offer plenty of suggestions, but the challenge is for you to take one step after another through the exercises ahead.

You might choose to use this workbook by yourself, with a friend, or in a small-group setting. (I provide suggestions for group use on pages xi–xiii). You might be someone who prefers to work through the exercises in one sitting, or you might choose to spread out the activities throughout the week. You might go back and forth between the book and the workbook, or you might complete them at separate times. My encouragement is to do whatever works best for you. I have created this workbook to be flexible and adaptable for your ideal use and benefit. If you invest yourself in these pages, you will find yourself a giant step closer to wholeness and healing after twelve weeks.

No doubt you come to this workbook struggling with depression. I tell you with absolute confidence that you don't have to live this way. You can be free to reach your highest potential. You can leave behind the weight on your shoulders that has been pressing down on you and move unencumbered and unconstrained toward a bright future.

Hundreds of my clients who have put the ideas in this workbook into practice are living proof that a whole new way of being is as near to you as your ability to hope. They have learned, as you can, that life need not be filled with depression, anxiety, regret, and fear. Every moment can be filled with wonder, exhilaration, optimism, and gratitude.

Start now.

Guidance for Groups

Healing can and does happen individually . . . but *most* healing happens within community. Depressed individuals often feel isolated, alone, and misunderstood. That's why groups centered on discussing depression and sharing personal experiences can be so powerful. Such groups are greatly needed because depression is recognized as one of the most widespread mental health issues in the world. Research reveals that

- in the last year, 10.3 million adults in the United States have experienced a depressive episode that caused some sort of severe impairment;
- almost half of those with a depression diagnosis have also been diagnosed with an anxiety disorder; and
- approximately 15 percent of US adults will experience depression during their lives.[1]

Despite the prevalence of depression, some people feel there's a stigma attached to this condition, as if they should "just get over it," have more faith, or act happy so they don't bring everyone else down with them. Worse, many depressed people feel deeply flawed at their core, falsely believing that their emotional struggles make them different from others, or even inferior.

A group centered on the topic of depression should, above all, seek to be loving, gracious, and accepting. Everyone on earth struggles with something, whether physical ailments, emotional problems, relationship disappointments, past traumas, spiritual disillusionment, addictive behaviors, and on and on. We are truly fellow travelers on the journey toward wholeness.

With this in mind, here are several suggestions for using this workbook effectively in a group setting:

- It's best for one person to serve as the facilitator, setting the tone for the gathering, guiding the discussion, and keeping the meeting focused.
- The facilitator should prepare ahead of time by reviewing the week's exercises and deciding which topics and questions would be appropriate and helpful within a group setting.
- Be sensitive to the discussion process. Try to give everyone an opportunity to speak, and when necessary, gently redirect the focus of those who tend to dominate a discussion.
- Be careful not to put anyone on the spot or make anyone feel pressured to share. The questions and assessments in this workbook cover some very personal and sensitive topics. Encourage group members to share their answers and thoughts if they feel comfortable doing so—and give them the freedom to stay quiet if they wish to.
- Use this workbook in conjunction with the *Healing Depression for Life* book, if possible. Ideally, the two go hand in hand, with the book providing thorough explanations of the whole-person approach and the workbook following up with practical exercises. However, each section of the workbook

begins with an "At a Glance" summary of the corresponding book-chapter content, followed by an "Essential Ideas" portion. So even those who have not read the book, or missed particular chapters, can get up to speed quickly and find the discussion helpful.

The sections of the workbook that best lend themselves to group discussion are "Essential Ideas . . . and Your Insights" and "Dig Deeper." Both of these sections include several questions and space for group members' responses. Some participants might like to share their journaling response from the "Change Your Story, Change Your Life" section. The bottom line is to use *any* of this material that will be most helpful in engaging your group members in the discussion process.

Finding a New Path Forward

Why Lasting Healing Can Feel like an Unreachable Mirage

Chapter 1 at a Glance

Here's an all-too-common response people get when they begin to admit they have a problem with depression: "It's all in your head! Just give it time." Or worse, "Snap out of it already!"

This kind of advice is rarely loving or helpful—though, like the broken clock that is accurate twice a day, it occasionally manages to be sort of right. That is, for people who are experiencing an ordinary case of the blues or temporary emotional upheaval due to grief or trauma, time can be an ally, and natural mental resiliency usually does return in due course.

But for millions of people around the world, those more common scenarios are unfamiliar. These individuals are caught in the grip of something larger and more tenacious than that. They suffer from clinical depression, and no amount of glib advice is going to make it "go away."

The fact is, depression is real. And painful. And frightening.

Too often, depression can even be life threatening when it drains a person of hope to the point of considering self-harm. Beyond the toll it takes on individual lives, depression places enormous strain on families, businesses, schools, and governments. In fact, no corner of society is immune to its disabling effects. That's true across the globe, not just in the United States.

But here's another vastly more important fact: depression is *not* a life sentence. Healing is possible, now and for good. After decades of treating scores of depressed people, I am convinced that genuine, lasting healing does not lie with any one solution. Chapter 1 of *Healing Depression for Life* examines common treatment options like antidepressant medications, talk therapy, and cognitive behavioral therapy and makes the case for the whole-person model we employ at The Center, which is a multifaceted combination of any and all avenues to healing.

Essential Ideas ... and Your Insights

1. **Depression is real—and won't go away without intentional action.** For the millions of people around the world battling depression, many of them (or most) have heard comments such as "It's a phase—you'll get over it" or "Dwell on positive thoughts and you'll feel better" or "You've got to have more faith in God. Overcome your doubts, and you'll overcome depression." The truth is, depression is painful, frightening, and sometimes life threatening. Depressed individuals are caught in the grip of a persistent and pervasive condition, and no amount of glib advice is going to make it "go away."

    Your response: Have you felt misunderstood—perhaps

you've received insensitive advice—as you've struggled with depression? What have you heard from others?

_____

_____

_____

_____

_____

2. **Many depressed people do nothing to address their condition
    … but they really should.** Among those battling depression,
    37 percent of adults and a staggering 60 percent of young people
    receive no treatment of any kind.[2] What's more, recent research
    has revealed that approximately one-third of people who do
    seek help receive little or no lasting benefit from treatments
    commonly used today.[3]

    Your response: Have you sought help for your depression?
    If so, how? What has been your experience with treatment
    options you have pursued?

    _____

    _____

    _____

    _____

    _____

3. **Depression is caused by multiple factors and should be
    treated with multiple approaches.** Most care providers
    recommend a single treatment (antidepressant medication,
    talk therapy, cognitive behavioral therapy, etc.) to address a
    disorder that is never caused by one thing alone. Depression
    is nearly always rooted in a variety of factors, sometimes
    going back years.

Your response: What is your perspective about treating depression with medication? Has someone (a health care provider, counselor, or friend) recommended a particular treatment for depression relief? If so, was it helpful?

_____

_____

_____

_____

_____

Taking Stock

Which of these approaches have you tried? And how much positive change have you experienced? Answer on a scale of 1 to 5, where 1 is "not very helpful" and 5 is "extremely helpful."

1. **Sleep Health:** Regular bedtime routine, at least seven hours of sleep nightly.

    1   2   3   4   5

2. **Limiting Use of Electronic Devices:** Taking several one-hour breaks each day, turning devices off at bedtime, setting aside devices for an entire day each week.

    1   2   3   4   5

3. **Stress Management:** Honestly assessing your stress level, seeking to reduce stress.

    1   2   3   4   5

4. **Addressing Hidden Addictions:** Recognizing your compulsive behaviors and seeking to overcome them.

    1   2   3   4   5

5. **Emotional Processing/Cleansing:** Addressing anger, guilt, and fear through counseling, journaling, and so on.

    1   2   3   4   5

6. **Forgiveness:** Intentionally addressing hurts and heartaches and releasing those who caused you harm.

    1   2   3   4   5

7. **Spiritual Practices:** Prayer, meditation, involvement in a faith community, reading sacred material, etc.

    1   2   3   4   5

8. **Physical movement:** At least thirty minutes of continuous exercise per day.

    1   2   3   4   5

9. **Fortifying Nutrition:** Reducing processed and sugary foods, consuming fruits and vegetables, using appropriate nutritional supplements and probiotics.

    1   2   3   4   5

10. **Detoxing Your Physical Body:** Regularly consuming antioxidant foods and beverages, abstaining from alcohol, etc.

    1   2   3   4   5

Change Your Story, Change Your Life

1. What is the story you tell yourself about depression? What is your self-talk about your condition (*I shouldn't feel this way . . . I just need to try harder and get over it . . . I'm a victim of my circumstances . . . Depression was passed down in my DNA . . . My painful childhood caused my*

depression . . .)? Write out your story—just let it flow without self-editing or filtering.

_____

_____

_____

_____

_____

_____

_____

_____

_____

_____

_____

2. Now write out a different narrative that you want to embrace. Where do you want to end up? Describe your ideal life, free from depression.

_____

_____

_____

_____

_____

_____

_____

_____

_____

_____

_____

Dig Deeper

1. What words would you use to describe depression (such as *heavy, burdensome, debilitating, confusing, enlightening, informative,* etc.)? Choose some descriptive words that are meaningful to you and write about their personal importance.

_____

_____

_____

_____

_____

2. What have you found to be helpful or unhelpful in relieving your depression? Describe your experience.

_____

_____

_____

_____

_____

3. What has been your most significant challenge related to your depression? This might be a practical issue (work productivity, attending to household tasks), an emotional issue (feeling misunderstood by others, struggling with self-esteem), or a spiritual issue (wondering where God is amid your painful experience).

_____

_____

_____

_____

_____

4. What insights have you gained because of your depression? Most people, understandably, are eager to move beyond depression. Yet this hardship has something to teach you. So, what have you learned from your experience?

_____

_____

_____

_____

_____

5. How do your spiritual beliefs intersect with your depression struggles? For example, do you feel the need to "have it all together" with your faith-oriented friends? Do you think you should just have "more faith" to prevail over your problems? Or do you rely on your spirituality as a source of strength? Describe your experience.

_____

_____

_____

_____

_____

First Steps, Next Steps

Now it's time to get practical. We've explored many issues that have prompted you to ponder and process. Let's put those thoughts into action. I'll provide several steps forward, and then it's your turn to determine three additional steps you will take this week.

1. Explore treatment options you might like to pursue. The whole-person approach my team and I advocate utilizes a

variety of tools that address emotional, physical, spiritual, and intellectual needs. Research options that begin with one aspect of healing that seems both safe and stretching to you. Write out your intention and plan to accomplish this step.

2. Talk with others who have struggled with depression about what has helped them. Reach out to friends, family members, or acquaintances with the questions "How have you dealt with depression? What worked for you?" Record your findings.

3. Recognize your resistance—and write about it. What is holding you back from looking honestly at your depression and seeking help? For example, most depressed people struggle to find energy and motivation to engage in actively seeking help. Others avoid painful emotional issues that contributed to depression. What, for you, is keeping you stuck?

4. Your turn. What steps do you intend to take this week to move toward wellness?

a. _____

_____

_____

b. _____

_____

_____

c. _____

_____

_____

Closing Reflections

You might be *struggling* with depression or *suffering* from depression. Whether struggling or suffering—or whatever other word you choose to describe your current condition—I want you to be assured of an essential truth: God wants you to experience healing. Depression has likely left you feeling isolated and alone in your pain. But you are not alone. God is with you.

The beloved pastor and author Charles Swindoll said, "No matter how dark the clouds, the sun will eventually pierce the darkness and dispel it; no matter how heavy the rain, the sun will ultimately prevail to hang a rainbow in the sky."[4]

Living in the Pacific Northwest, where rainstorms are frequent occurrences, I have witnessed many amazing rainbows. Double rainbows of vibrant, multicolored arches paint the sky at the smallest hint of sunshine after a drenching downpour. When I see them, I smile, believing in the promise they deliver. I believe in their confirmation of a loving God who announces the sun after the rain with such exuberant celebration.

Do you know that God wants you to experience the same celebration of healing in your life? He wants the sunshine to break through the dark clouds of your depression. From the dreariness and darkness of your pain, God wants to send forth his rainbow of healing and bring you joy so you can experience once again the fullness and joyfulness he intended for you all along.

Scripture for Meditation

Life will be brighter than noonday,
    and darkness will become like morning.
You will be secure, because there is hope;
    you will look about you and take your rest in safety.
JOB 11:17-18

Wise Words to Awaken Your Spirit

The most beautiful people we have known are those who have known defeat, known suffering, known struggle, known loss, and have found their way out of the depths. These persons have an appreciation, a sensitivity, and an understanding of life that fills them with compassion, gentleness, and a deep loving concern. Beautiful people do not just happen.
ELISABETH KÜBLER-ROSS

Journal Your Journey

This week you are going to be trying out new things, taking steps forward, forging new habits, and letting go of old ones. Will these things make a difference? Will you be able to discern any changes in how you feel and what you think?

This page is here for you to journal about the journey. What works? What doesn't? You'll know what to keep doing because you'll have your adventure documented in the pages of this workbook. Use this space to ask questions, make lists, doodle, write about your progress, and record milestones.

Let the adventure begin!

Sound Asleep

The Curative Power of a Solid Night's Sleep

Chapter 2 at a Glance

The link between depression and sadness is common knowledge; the relationship between depression and fatigue or stress or grief is also familiar ground. What you don't hear as much about is the link between depression and sleep. And yet, after working with literally thousands of clients, I can tell you that when someone is struggling with depression, sleep challenges are virtually always part of the problem, and addressing those challenges must be part of the solution.

When we don't get enough sleep, the impact on our brains, bodies, and emotions is profound. Without adequate sleep, for example, there is decreased overall activity in the brain, which compromises how we perform at cognitive tasks like learning, remembering, paying attention, being productive, and even driving.

Not getting enough sleep also interferes with how well our bodies function and heal. Heart health is compromised, as is the body's ability to repair injuries to joints and muscles. Even weight is impacted, since when we don't get enough sleep, our bodies produce less of the hormone that controls appetite, meaning we eat more (and weigh more too!).

Furthermore, the link between sleep and emotional well-being can't be ignored. More than ever before, researchers are documenting a disturbing correlation between depression and sleep problems. Nearly nine out of ten people with severe depression also suffer from insomnia.

In fact, sleep studies show that depression actually changes our sleep architecture.[5] There is some debate over which comes first—sleep disturbances or depression—but there is no debate that each fuels the other, creating a downward spiral.

Essential Ideas ... and Your Insights

1. **If you struggle with getting a solid night's sleep, you're not alone.** Studies show that more than a third of adults and more than two-thirds of teenagers do not get enough sleep.[6] Much of the problem is attributed to the rise in the use of personal technology at night. As it turns out, using cell phones right before falling asleep is both physiologically and psychologically stimulating and activates the brain in ways that noninteractive media don't. In fact, the decline in sleep quality is so widespread, it's been called nothing short of an epidemic.

   Your response: Do you struggle with sleep problems? Can you identify some of the factors keeping you from getting a good night's sleep? Do you use technology before bedtime? If so, how might this be impacting the quality of your sleep?

---

2. **Depression and sleep issues go hand in hand.** The relationship between sleep and depression is so profound that I have most of my incoming clients undergo sleep studies. If you are depressed and sleep deprived, these two dynamics are fueling each other, and the cycle must be disrupted if you are to find relief.

    Your response: What effects do you experience the day after not getting enough sleep? Do you believe sleep disturbances are having a negative impact on your emotions? What do you think is the correlation between your sleep problems and your depression?

    _____

    _____

    _____

    _____

3. **When sleep issues are addressed, symptoms of depression decrease.** If you've been trying to abolish depression without success, make a concerted effort to address your sleep issues. Because these dynamics are working together, addressing either one can help break the cycle. If you can improve the quality of your sleep, your mental and emotional health will improve as well.

    Your response: Are you encouraged to know that sleeping better can give you relief from depression? Do you feel optimistic or pessimistic about improving your sleep? What is one thing you can do to improve your sleep tonight?

    _____

    _____

    _____

    _____

Taking Stock

Studies show that engaging in the following behaviors can help us sleep better. How often do you do these behaviors? 1 = not very often; 2 = often but not regularly; 3 = every day.

1. Spend time outside to benefit from natural light
      1   2   3

2. Exercise
      1   2   3

3. Stay away from heavy, rich, or spicy food close to bedtime
      1   2   3

4. Avoid electronics close to bedtime
      1   2   3

5. Keep your cell phone put away or in another room at night
      1   2   3

6. Follow relaxing evening rituals to wind down for bedtime
      1   2   3

7. Keep your room as dark as possible
      1   2   3

8. Avoid lying awake in bed at night
      1   2   3

9. Before going to sleep, empty your mind of tomorrow's to-dos by making a list
      1   2   3

How many of these activities do you engage in regularly? Which ones might you try next?

Change Your Story, Change Your Life

1. What is the story you tell yourself about your relationship with sleep? Do you tell yourself you just can't sleep? Are you resigned to struggle the rest of your life? Do you think sleep problems are an unavoidable aspect of your life and change is impossible, or do you have hope that you will find a solution one day? Write out your story—just let it flow without self-editing or filtering.

_____

_____

_____

_____

_____

_____

2. Now write out a different narrative you want to embrace. Where do you want to end up? Describe your ideal relationship with sleep.

_____

_____

_____

_____

_____

_____

Dig Deeper

1. What does sleep represent to you? Do you dread going to bed at night or look forward to it? Why do you think sleep has these associations for you?

   _____

   _____

   _____

   _____

   _____

2. In the past, what things have you tried that have had a positive impact on the quality of your sleep? Do you do these things regularly? If not, why not?

   _____

   _____

   _____

   _____

   _____

3. How committed are you to taking actions to improve your sleep? Are there habits you've known would help you sleep better but you have put off embracing these habits? If so, why?

   _____

   _____

   _____

   _____

   _____

4. Are you a workaholic? Have you bought into the idea that you are somehow a more dynamic, productive, or responsible person if you consistently sacrifice sleep to get things done? Is this a healthy attitude to have? What would you tell a friend who had this mind-set and, as a result, was struggling with sleep problems and depression?

    _____

    _____

    _____

    _____

    _____

5. Do a search of verses in the Bible that deal with rest. If you do an online search of "Bible verses about rest," you will find lists of twenty to thirty verses. Read them through and write your thoughts below.

    _____

    _____

    _____

    _____

    _____

First Steps, Next Steps

Now it's time to get practical. We've explored many issues that prompted you to ponder and process. Let's put those thoughts into action. I'll provide several steps forward, and then it's your turn to determine three additional actions you will take this week.

1. Take a good look at your habits in the hour or two before bedtime. Evaluate what you eat, how you're using technology,

and whether you follow a relaxing wind-down sequence of actions. What changes can you make?

---

2. Evaluate your bedroom. Name three things you can do today to help you sleep better tonight (for example, remove clutter, put fresh sheets on your bed, make your bedroom darker by removing electronics that are emitting light).

---

3. Motivate yourself with a good, old-fashioned list of pros and cons. Draw a line down the middle of a sheet of paper. On the left side of the line, write the negative things you experience when you don't get enough sleep. On the right side of the line, write the benefits you experience when you feel fully rested.

---

4. Your turn. What steps do you intend to take this week to move toward wellness?

a. _____

_____

_____

b. _____

_____

_____

c. _____

_____

_____

Closing Reflections

God wants you to rest. In fact, rest is so foundational to your mental, emotional, physical, and spiritual well-being that God has instructed you to take an entire day of rest—the Sabbath—*every week*.

I believe taking a weekly day of rest gives us a chance to practice laying aside stress and distractions, a skill we can also put to good use each night as we lay aside the cares of the day. Rest is restorative. Sleep is restorative.

In our love affair with productivity, it's tempting to sacrifice rest and sleep on the altar of "doing things." And yet God designed us to need rest and sleep and, in fact, to thrive when we are intentional about creating space in our lives for these things.

Scripture for Meditation

In vain you rise early
　　and stay up late,
toiling for food to eat—
　　for he grants sleep to those he loves.

PSALM 127:2

Wise Words to Awaken Your Spirit

Sleep is that golden chain that ties health and our bodies together.

THOMAS DEKKER

Journal Your Journey

This week you are going to be trying out new things, taking steps forward, forging new habits, and letting go of old ones. Will these things make a difference? Will you be able to discern any changes in how you feel and what you think?

This page is here for you to journal about the journey. What works? What doesn't? You'll know what to keep doing because you'll have your adventure documented in the pages of this workbook. Use this space to ask questions, make lists, doodle, write about your progress, and record milestones.

Let the adventure begin!

Your Devices, Your Depression

*How Overuse of Technology
Erodes Mental Health*

Chapter 3 at a Glance

According to ongoing research, the link between the use of modern technology and depression is . . . complicated. While some studies indicate clear cause-and-effect relationships between depressive symptoms and too much time spent online or engaged in social media, others are less conclusive.

In some ways, that's to be expected when studying something that's so new. Widespread social media use, for instance, is still not even a few decades old. The hypothesized effects of too much screen time are also largely subjective and difficult to measure. It's hard to get definitive answers when we're still not entirely sure what the right questions are.

And yet I can confirm from firsthand experience—after working with hundreds of clients over several decades—that the misuse of technology has a direct impact on the severity of depressive symptoms. It's why I have made addressing this behavior a key part of the whole-person approach to healing. When we ask people to put away their devices as treatment begins, it doesn't take long for signs of distress and even addiction to appear.

The key to understanding the dilemma lies in the words *misuse* and *too much*. There is no need to fear technology itself. We all know it can be an amazing asset and convenience in our lives. But how we use it is of great importance to anyone determined to heal from depression. Finding balance is a checkpoint we can't afford to ignore. Changing your relationship to the Internet is a big step on the road to getting there.

Essential Ideas … and Your Insights

1. **Technology in itself is not good or bad—it's how we use it that matters.** We need to be wise in the use of our devices because they can become more unhelpful than helpful. Fire can cook your food or burn down your house, depending on how you employ it. Ultimately, that's good news. It suggests that whether your use of technology is harmful or beneficial is mostly up to you.

    Your response: What is your personal perspective on technology and its place in our society? Do you love it, hate it, or have mixed feelings? Why?

    ----

2. **There is a direct correlation between the misuse of technology and depression.** Numerous research studies

demonstrate technology's adverse effects when it is not utilized appropriately—that is, without clear limits and boundaries. And I can confirm from my work with clients that the misuse of technology has a direct impact on the severity of depressive symptoms. That's why addressing this behavior is a key component of healing depression.

Your response: Before beginning this session, had you considered how technology misuse contributes to your mood? How does this prompt you to rethink your use of electronic devices?

_____

_____

_____

_____

3. **Technology has an addictive quality.** At the heart of any addiction is impulse control—the struggle to say no to something that could have negative consequences. If you are battling depression, this is a big problem. A common response to the distress of depression is to reach for anything that makes you "feel better." With the world at your fingertips via the Internet, the range of self-medication options is practically endless.

Your response: Do you believe that technology can be addictive in the way that substances like drugs and alcohol can be? In what ways can technology be used by depressed people to self-medicate?

_____

_____

_____

_____

Taking Stock

Often the biggest hurdle to dealing with an addiction to technology is denial that a problem exists. The following questions will help you self-assess the depth of your dependence on technology and reveal what that may be costing you.

1. Does it make you nervous to be separated from one or more of your devices?

   YES / NO

2. Are you focused on a screen (computer, phone, tablet, TV) for more than two hours a day for reasons other than work?

   YES / NO

3. Do you often lose sleep because you can't disconnect from an online activity at bedtime?

   YES / NO

4. Do you turn down opportunities to do other things if participation means stepping away from technology?

   YES / NO

5. Do you feel anxious at the thought of spending an entire weekend offline?

   YES / NO

6. Do you send more than twenty-five texts in a day?

   YES / NO

7. Do your friends and family complain about your use of devices?

   YES / NO

8. Does the thought of missing out on something important if you unplug, even for a moment, make you anxious?
YES / NO

9. Do you routinely text while driving or walking?
YES / NO

10. Do you often immediately interrupt other activities (work, meals, conversations with others, etc.) when a message arrives?
YES / NO

11. Do you often feel physically drained after lengthy periods of time online?
YES / NO

12. Do you skip meals when spending time online?
YES / NO

If you answered yes to any of these questions, it might be time to reassess the role of technology in your life. If you answered yes to more than half of them, you do not control your devices—they control you. It's time to take action.

Change Your Story, Change Your Life

1. What is the story you tell yourself about your relationship with technology? Depending on the era you grew up in, you might feel perfectly comfortable with all kinds of technology—or fairly uncomfortable. Describe your feelings and approach. Consider your use of technology over the years as it relates

to your depression. Write out your story—just let it flow without self-editing or filtering.

2. Now write out a different narrative you want to embrace. Where do you want to end up? Describe your ideal relationship with technology.

Dig Deeper

1. What do you think are the helpful and the unhelpful aspects of the widespread use of technology in our society in general?

2. What do you think are the helpful and the unhelpful aspects of technology use for *you*?

_____

_____

_____

_____

_____

_____

3. Imagine living in the era when your grandparents or great-grandparents lived, without computers, smartphones, iPads, or the Internet. Does that simpler lifestyle appeal to you, make you feel edgy, or both? Why?

_____

_____

_____

_____

_____

_____

4. What are some specific ways you can put healthy limits and boundaries around your use of technology?

_____

_____

_____

_____

_____

5. Is there someone in your life whose misuse or overuse of technology concerns you? What would you like to say to that

person? How would your words of concern to the other person apply to yourself?

First Steps, Next Steps

Now it's time to get practical. We've explored many issues that prompted you to ponder and process. Let's put those thoughts into action. I'll provide several steps forward, and then it's your turn to determine three additional actions you will take this week.

1. Review the ideas you came up with for limiting technology use. Begin to implement those strategies this week. Describe how you will do this.

2. Look at chapter 3 of *Healing Depression for Life*, specifically the section called "Hidden Costs" (which includes addiction, isolation, virtual conflict, physical stagnation, and other possible consequences of tech misuse—see pages 34–42).

Identify which of these particularly apply to you, and describe ways you can counteract these hidden costs.

_____

_____

_____

_____

_____

3. Write out specific ways you can put yourself on a "tech diet" (such as a limited time period for social media, a daily tech time-out for a few hours, a day of the week without electronic devices, and so on).

_____

_____

_____

_____

_____

4. Your turn. What steps do you intend to take this week to move toward wellness?

a. _____

_____

_____

b. _____

_____

_____

c. _____

_____

_____

Closing Reflections

Sometimes being abnormal is a good thing. And sometimes being a nonconformist can lead to healing. As pastor Craig Groeschel says, "Normal people live distracted, rarely fully present. Weird people silence the distractions and remain fully in the moment."[7]

The fact is, we are the most distracted people in history. From the moment we wake in the morning, our minds are pulled in every direction—work deadlines, household tasks, family demands, and financial concerns. But of course in our modern era we are most distracted by our electronic devices. The average person spends more time using electronic gadgets than doing anything else. For most people, the majority of the day is spent using a computer, watching TV, talking and texting on a smartphone, or playing video games.

Our devices distract us from the real issues of life and move us away from important opportunities. As a society, we have largely lost our appreciation for quietness and introspection. It is in moments of tranquility that we allow our imaginations the freedom to conceive new ideas. It is in moments of contemplation that we listen for spiritual guidance. It is in moments of unhurried reflection that we come to understand who we are as unique individuals.

The good news is that distraction is not inevitable. Distraction is a habit, nothing more. We have been *conditioned* to use our devices nonstop, but we can also be *re*conditioned to use them selectively. So set aside time this week—a few minutes or a few hours each day—to turn off all devices. Use the time to pray and reflect. Meditate on a meaningful Scripture passage. Be quiet and listen for the Spirit of God speaking to you.

Scripture for Meditation

"I have the right to do anything," you say—but not everything is beneficial. "I have the right to do anything"—but I will not be mastered by anything.

1 CORINTHIANS 6:12

Wise Words to Awaken Your Spirit

Technology is the knack of so arranging the world that we do not experience it.

ROLLO MAY

Journal Your Journey

This week you are going to be trying out new things, taking steps forward, forging new habits, and letting go of old ones. Will these things make a difference? Will you be able to discern any changes in how you feel and what you think?

This page is here for you to journal about the journey. What works? What doesn't? You'll know what to keep doing because you'll have your adventure documented in the pages of this workbook. Use this space to ask questions, make lists, doodle, write about your progress, and record milestones.

Let the adventure begin!

Stressed and Depressed

How to Tame Chronic Stress and Regain Emotional Wellness

Chapter 4 at a Glance

Low-level stress is actually a good thing, boosting brain activity, concentration, and productivity. Low-level stress is also a big motivator to make positive changes in your life.

The problem with stress arises when we are subjected to constant, chronic stress. Constant stress messes with our bodies, our emotions, and our thoughts and is linked to all sorts of detrimental health and mental issues, which is why making changes to reduce your level of ongoing stress is a great idea.

Identifying the sources of your stress is always a good place to start. Then, armed with this list, make an action plan to reduce stressors in your life or to deal more effectively with stress. (And as you are putting your plan into action, if you fall back into old habits, cut yourself some slack. Forgive yourself and move on.)

Reducing stress—especially ongoing, chronic stress—is critical if you struggle with depression. Studies have proven that chronic stress triggers conditions and processes in our bodies that make us more prone to depression, even years after the stressful event has passed.

The problem with chronic stress is that it creates a condition of systemic inflammation in our bodies. This kind of inflammation is linked to chronic pain, Alzheimer's disease, cancer, diabetes, depression, and more.[8]

Essential Ideas ... and Your Insights

1. **Stress increases depression because it tempts us to abandon good habits and embrace bad ones.** If you've struggled with depression, you may have realized that embracing certain healthy habits has a positive impact on your mental and emotional health. In fact, behaviors like getting enough sleep, eating right, and getting exercise are proven to be depression deterrents. So what's the first thing we do when we feel stressed? Lose sleep, eat comfort food, and skip the gym. No wonder stress is so strongly linked with depression!

   Your response: What habits and behaviors help you deal with depression? When you are stressed, are you tempted to abandon any of your good habits? Which ones? Does stress ever drive you to unhealthy coping behaviors? Give some examples.

   _____

   _____

   _____

   _____

2. **Ongoing, chronic stress triggers inflammation, which causes depression and many other ills.** Stress and depression are linked by more than bad habits vs. good habits. Ongoing,

chronic stress creates inflammation throughout your body, and that systemic inflammation causes a wide spectrum of ills . . . including depression.

Your response: Ongoing, chronic stress is a real game changer (in a negative way) when it comes to your physical, emotional, and mental health. Do you live in a constant state of stress? How long has this been going on? Can you pinpoint the source(s) of this ongoing stress? How does it affect your body, mind, and emotions?

_____

_____

_____

_____

3. **Take control of what you can control.** Stress in life is inevitable, and some stress is a necessary ingredient if we want to accomplish things and grow as individuals. But ongoing, chronic stress is never good and needs to be addressed. One of the ways to reduce the impact of stress in your life is to learn to take control of what you can control—and let go of the rest.

Your response: Is part of your stress due to always trying (unsuccessfully) to control things that are really out of your control? What concerns keep you awake at night, despite the fact that you can't influence the outcome? At the same time, are you stressed because you haven't taken care of things that *are* within your control?

_____

_____

_____

_____

Taking Stock

HOW STRESSED ARE YOU?

Place a check mark beside any of the symptoms you experience continually:

- O Neck and jaw pain from clenching or grinding teeth
- O Difficulty concentrating
- O Feeling overwhelmed
- O Frequent bouts of crying
- O Insomnia and/or disturbing dreams
- O Heartburn, stomach pain, excessive belching
- O Diarrhea and/or constipation
- O Feelings of anxiety or nervousness
- O Fatigue
- O Irritability
- O Chronic pain
- O Changes in libido, with a decreased interest in sex
- O Rapid heart rate
- O Changes in appetite, such as overeating or loss of appetite

When you are in a stressful situation, you can experience any combination of the symptoms above for a season. That's common and normal for all of us. But if you are experiencing even a few of these symptoms on an ongoing basis, it's likely that chronic stress is the culprit. Reducing your levels of stress should be a top priority.

Change Your Story, Change Your Life

1. What is the story you tell yourself about your relationship with stress? How often do you feel overwhelmed and stressed? What

do you do when you feel this way? Write out your story—just let it flow without self-editing or filtering.

_____

_____

_____

_____

_____

_____

2. Now write out a different narrative you want to embrace. Where do you want to end up? Remembering that stress is a part of life and can even be a powerful motivator, write about your ideal relationship with stress.

_____

_____

_____

_____

_____

_____

Dig Deeper

1. Do you think of yourself as a victim, or are there things you are doing that contribute to the stress that you feel? Which of your choices, behaviors, or expectations are adding to your stress?

_____

_____

_____

_____

2. Do you procrastinate? Does your procrastination add to your stress? How?

_____

_____

_____

_____

3. What are your go-to sources of relief when you are feeling stress? Are these coping strategies reducing your stress or adding to it?

_____

_____

_____

_____

4. Are you in any relationships that are contributing to your levels of stress? What can you do to reduce the stress associated with these individuals? List your options. Put a check by several that you are willing to explore.

_____

_____

_____

_____

5. Do you have someone you can talk to about the stress in your life? Who? Why did you pick this person with whom you can be completely honest?

_____

_____

_____

_____

First Steps, Next Steps

Now it's time to get practical. We've explored many issues that prompted you to ponder and process. Let's put those thoughts into action. I'll provide several steps forward, and then it's your turn to determine three additional actions you will take this week.

1. If procrastination or inefficient ways of getting things done are adding to your stress, there are many productivity tools that can help. Read a book on productivity or organization and see if there are one or more strategies you can adopt that will lessen your stress. Record what you find here.

    ----

2. Make a list of healthy ways to cope with stress. Ideas on your list might include taking a walk, praying, practicing deep breathing, expressing gratitude, solving a problem, talking with a friend, doing something nice for someone else, listening to music, or playing with a dog. The next time you are feeling stressed, do one thing from your list.

    ----

3. Evaluate your diet. Eating wisely when stressed isn't always easy, but you'll be glad you did. Make a list of five foods that call your name when you are stressed, then five alternative foods (or activities) you can choose instead.

    _____

    _____

    _____

    _____

    _____

4. Your turn. What steps do you intend to take this week to move toward wellness?

    a. _____

    _____

    _____

    b. _____

    _____

    _____

    c. _____

    _____

    _____

Closing Reflections

Are your thoughts adding to your stress? When life feels overwhelming, it's easy to tell ourselves things that are not only untrue but also unhelpful, adding to our anxiety and stress. We might think, *This wouldn't be happening if I were a better person . . . Things will never get better . . . Why do these things always happen to me? . . . I have no control over my life.*

Replace thoughts like these with positive alternatives, such as, *I am strong enough to get through this tough situation . . . God is willing and eager to help me . . . Life is hard, but I can handle anything that's thrown at me . . . I can control how I respond to unexpected circumstances.*

Your faith in God is one of the most effective stress-reducers available to you. In fact, studies show that going to church, praying, and believing in God are linked with improved mental health.[9]

So the next time you find yourself feeling stressed, take a deep breath and remember the words of King Solomon, the wisest man in history: "Trust in the LORD with all your heart and lean not on your own understanding" (Proverbs 3:5).

Scripture for Meditation

Come to me, all of you who are weary and carry heavy burdens, and I will give you rest.

MATTHEW 11:28, NLT

Wise Words to Awaken Your Spirit

The greatest weapon against stress is our ability to choose one thought over another.

WILLIAM JAMES

Journal Your Journey

This week you are going to be trying out new things, taking steps forward, forging new habits, and letting go of old ones. Will these things make a difference? Will you be able to discern any changes in how you feel and what you think?

This page is here for you to journal about the journey. What works? What doesn't? You'll know what to keep doing because you'll have your adventure documented in the pages of this workbook.

Use this space to ask questions, make lists, doodle, write about your progress, and record milestones.

Let the adventure begin!

A Hard Look at Hard Issues

Uncovering Hidden Addictions Can Set You Free

Chapter 5 at a Glance

Say you want to sail across the ocean. If at the moment of departure you can't or don't raise the anchor, it won't matter how well you've prepared. You aren't going anywhere.

That perfectly describes how some people approach healing from depression. Initially, they do the hard work of changing what they eat, improving their sleep habits, eliminating environmental toxins, addressing emotional baggage, and even forgiving those who've harmed them in some way—all the things that make up our whole-person treatment model. But at the end of the day, none of that is enough to set them free from depression, because something extraordinarily dense and heavy keeps them stuck in the mud.

They are tethered to the anchor of *addiction*.

This is so common, in fact, that at any given time as many as 40 percent of people at The Center seeking help with depression are concurrently enrolled in another of our major treatment programs—addiction rehab. In some ways, these people are the lucky ones, because their dependence on drugs or alcohol, or both, has become so apparent that they can no longer deny the obvious need for help. At the other end of the spectrum, however, are people whose addictions are easier to hide—even from themselves. They have become dependent on behaviors that are legal and often considered "normal" in modern society and therefore harmless. Don't be fooled, though; these behaviors are just as heavy and just as likely to prevent you from making headway on your journey to healing.

The good news is, if you confront your addictions—large and small—you'll lift a weight from your shoulders and make success that much more attainable.

Essential Ideas . . . and Your Insights

1. **Addictions cover a wide array of behaviors.** These include everything from debilitating drug or alcohol use to out-of-control gambling, along with so-called "soft" addictions such as shopping, video game playing, and codependent relationships. In all cases, the working definition of addiction is the same: *continued compulsive substance use or behavior despite harmful consequences.* If an action repeatedly has an adverse effect on your life but you can't or won't stop, then you are most likely addicted.

   Your response: How do you react to this definition of addiction, particularly regarding any of your own behaviors? As you consider your lifestyle, are there red flags that cause concern about compulsive or addictive behaviors?

   _____

   _____

   _____

   _____

2. **An addiction of any kind will alter your mood.** And that is precisely what people want to do when feeling depressed— change their mood. Since compulsive involvement with addictive substances or activities usually brings temporary relief, pleasure, or even bliss, it's not surprising that depressed individuals return to these behaviors again and again. Quite often, they pursue the harmful habits more intensely and more frequently to achieve the same mood elevation and sense of relief.

   Your response: How would you describe the link between addictive behaviors and mood swings? Sometimes it's easy to see how addictions affect moods (alcohol, drugs, caffeine), but how do you think harder-to-detect compulsive behaviors (shopping, overworking, unhealthy relationships) can influence depression?

   _____

   _____

   _____

   _____

   _____

3. **Compulsive behaviors do nothing to address the real causes of depression.** In fact, they only mask them and distract from them. One of the points I stress over and over is that depression almost never goes away on its own. What's more, depression typically gets worse if a person doesn't explore the root issues—and especially if habits and patterns persist that contribute to mood imbalance.

   Your response: In what ways do you think compulsive behaviors distract from, or even prevent, the healing of depression? Describe in your own words the interconnection between addictions and depression.

_____

_____

_____

_____

_____

Taking Stock

Addictions to a wide variety of substances and behaviors are like a ball and chain that keep us stuck in depression. Breaking addiction is an indispensable step in healing.

Label the following statements never/sometimes/always. Take an honest look at what you discover.

1. I keep doing _____ in spite of clear negative consequences.
   NEVER / SOMETIMES / ALWAYS

2. I experience psychological and/or physical withdrawal when I try to stop doing it.
   NEVER / SOMETIMES / ALWAYS

3. I avoid activities and social situations where I'm unable to do it.
   NEVER / SOMETIMES / ALWAYS

4. I try hard to keep my habit a secret from others, including lying to people I care about.
   NEVER / SOMETIMES / ALWAYS

5. I have lost the ability to say no to myself.
   NEVER / SOMETIMES / ALWAYS

6. It takes more of the substance or activity to make me feel satisfied or relieved than it used to.
   NEVER / SOMETIMES / ALWAYS

7. I take risks and make serious sacrifices in order to do it.
   NEVER / SOMETIMES / ALWAYS

8. I feel defensive when someone expresses concern that something is not right.
   NEVER / SOMETIMES / ALWAYS

9. I feel I need this activity just to get through the day.
   NEVER / SOMETIMES / ALWAYS

10. Doing this thing makes me feel guilty or ashamed.
    NEVER / SOMETIMES / ALWAYS

If you answered mostly "sometimes" and "always," then you are very likely struggling with an addiction. The next questions will help you firm up your determination to be free.

I keep doing this thing because it makes me feel . . .

    1.

    2.

    3.

    4.

I need what this thing makes me feel because . . .

    1.

    2.

    3.

    4.

I can meet that need differently by . . .

    1.

    2.

    3.

    4.

If _____ were not a part of my life, I would
    be better off because . . .

    1.

    2.

    3.

    4.

I would rather do the work of getting free than stay stuck
    because . . .

    1.

    2.

    3.

    4.

Change Your Story, Change Your Life

1. What is the story you tell yourself about your relationship
   with compulsive behaviors? If you are struggling with harmful
   behaviors (even if not a diagnosed addiction), what is your
   history with this issue? How did it evolve in your life? Have you
   resigned yourself to struggle the rest of your life? Write out your
   story—just let it flow without self-editing or filtering.

_____

_____

_____

_____

_____

2. Now write out a different narrative you want to embrace. Where do you want to end up? Describe your ideal relationship with addiction.

_____

_____

_____

_____

_____

Dig Deeper

1. In *Healing Depression for Life*, I emphasize that many people resist admitting they have an addiction because of the stigma attached to it, often perpetuated by media images and portrayals of addicts. What do you think is involved in this stigma, and how exactly does it prevent taking an honest look at harmful behaviors?

_____

_____

_____

_____

2. Many people try to overcome depression while leaving
    addictive behavior unaddressed. This simply doesn't work. As I
    say in the book, "Facing and overcoming addiction of any kind
    is absolutely necessary to healing depression." Why do you
    think this is? In your opinion, how is addiction a roadblock to
    recovery from depression?

    _____

    _____

    _____

    _____

    _____

3. What is your perspective on "process addictions" (also called
    "soft addictions"), which include issues such as codependent
    relationships and compulsive shopping, eating, gambling,
    hoarding, and even exercising? Many people minimize these
    problems because they begin as normal behaviors—but they
    become uncontrollable. How do you think these conditions
    contribute to a person's depression?

    _____

    _____

    _____

    _____

    _____

4. Shame and guilt are almost always present within someone
    battling an addiction. When a person is harboring a secret
    addiction, then shame and guilt lead directly to feeling
    powerless, worthless, and unlovable—all the hallmarks of
    entrenched depression. Describe how you believe these two

powerful emotions keep someone stuck in addiction and spiraling into depression.

5. Are you currently dealing with an addiction? Do you see how this behavior is deepening your depression? Is there something that is keeping you from addressing this issue?

First Steps, Next Steps

Now it's time to get practical. We've explored many issues that prompted you to ponder and process. Let's put those thoughts into action. I'll provide several steps forward, and then it's your turn to determine three additional actions you will take this week.

1. Complete a thorough addiction evaluation. Do this even if you believe compulsive behavior is not a problem for you. The process is informative, and many people are surprised at the results. The "Taking Stock" assessment in this chapter is a good start, but you can also pursue a more in-depth assessment from a health care provider who specializes in

addiction treatment. Describe your plan and commitment to complete this step.

_____

_____

_____

_____

2. Look back at chapter 5 of *Healing Depression for Life*, particularly the subsection called "What's It Got to Do with Depression?" (see pages 62–64). There I describe the typical sequence of actions and feelings that come along with addiction: secrecy, deception, shame and guilt, and further self-medication. Write about your experience with any or all of these aspects (whether or not you struggle with addiction).

_____

_____

_____

_____

3. Enlist an accountability/encouragement partner. Find someone you trust and talk through the issue of addiction and depression. This might be a counselor, pastor, or friend. Speak honestly to determine if you need to seek more help for addiction issues. Write out your steps for moving forward.

_____

_____

_____

_____

4. Your turn. What steps do you intend to take this week to move toward wellness?

a. _____

_____

_____

b. _____

_____

_____

c. _____

_____

_____

Closing Reflections

One of my favorite Scriptures, as a person of faith and as a mental health expert, contains the words of Jesus: "Know the truth, and the truth will set you free" (John 8:32). This simple phrase is full of profound and life-changing wisdom. I have seen this principle lived out countless times in my counseling with struggling people: those who are willing to confront the truth, however painful, usually end up finding freedom and healing. Sadly, those who avoid the truth make little progress.

The unfortunate fact is that people caught in the grip of addiction have trouble accepting the truth and telling the truth. They keep the truth from themselves, remaining in denial about the severity of their condition. They keep the truth from loved ones, hiding things and acting secretively. They might also keep the truth from God, avoiding honest conversations and confession.

If you want to heal your depression for life, you must confront any addictions you're battling . . . and this always begins with the truth. When total honesty becomes your way of living and relating, you'll discover benefits in every facet of your life. The more truth, the less stress you'll experience. The more truth, the fewer sleepless nights you'll endure. The more truth, the closer your relationships will be. The more truth, the deeper inner peace you will enjoy. Live the truth, and you will find the freedom you've been seeking.

Scripture for Meditation

No temptation has overtaken you except what is common to mankind. And God is faithful; he will not let you be tempted beyond what you can bear. But when you are tempted, he will also provide a way out so that you can endure it.

1 CORINTHIANS 10:13

Wise Words to Awaken Your Spirit

A deep sense of love and belonging is an irreducible need of all people. We are biologically, cognitively, physically, and spiritually wired to love, to be loved, and to belong. When those needs are not met, we don't function as we were meant to. We break. We fall apart. We numb. We ache. We hurt others. We get sick.

BRENÉ BROWN

Journal Your Journey

This week you are going to be trying out new things, taking steps forward, forging new habits, and letting go of old ones. Will these things make a difference? Will you be able to discern any changes in how you feel and what you think?

This page is here for you to journal about the journey. What works? What doesn't? You'll know what to keep doing because you'll have your adventure documented in the pages of this workbook.

Use this space to ask questions, make lists, doodle, write about your progress, and record milestones.

Let the adventure begin!

The Three Deadly Emotions

How Unresolved Anger, Guilt, and Fear Undermine Healing

Chapter 6 at a Glance

Like the three witches in Shakespeare's *Macbeth*, there is a trio of emotions within each of us that, if left unchecked, can poison our minds and lives. They go hand in hand—with an uncanny ability to fuel one another—and are nearly always present to some degree in the hearts and minds of people suffering from depression.

They are anger, guilt, and fear—the three deadly emotions.

Here's the bottom line: lasting healing is simply not possible when unexamined and untended anger, guilt, and fear smolder beneath the surface of your life. They will undermine any progress made on other fronts—such as nutrition, sleep, and exercise—and place a hard limit on what's possible. For this reason, while some traditional treatments for depression ignore these emotions, the whole-person model makes diffusing them a high priority, just as important as any other link in the chain of healing.

The good news about overheated emotions is that you need not live as their hostage. It is possible to regain the upper hand over what you feel and why. It's understandable if your first reaction is to doubt that claim. Chances are, you've been living with deadly anger, guilt, and fear for so long that they seem woven into your very personality. Don't despair! This is not true. With discipline and concentrated effort—and with support from professionals and others in your life who are willing to help—you will see a dramatic change when you set out to tame your emotions.

Essential Ideas . . . and Your Insights

1. **Unaddressed anger, guilt, and fear act as fuel on the fire of depression.** It is difficult to say which comes first, runaway deadly emotions or depression. But in any case, they have a proven and powerfully negative influence on one another. If you are prone to depression for other reasons, these toxic feelings will rob you of the natural resilience you need to keep or regain your balance.

    Your response: How have these three emotions been present in your life over the past decade? In what ways have anger, guilt, and fear contributed to your depression?

    _____

    _____

    _____

    _____

2. **The emotions often labeled as "negative and bad" can, in fact, be "positive and good."** We won't come any closer to healing depression if we simply brand anger, guilt, and fear as undesirable and attempt to bury them away.

Like everything else, even emotions that can have such a deadly effect on mental and physical health may also play a positive role in our lives. There are two sides to every coin. In this case, the trick is in seeing the fundamental difference between the side of our emotions that leads to the darkness of depression and the side that is healthy and life giving.

Your response: Given your upbringing (family modeling, religious instruction, early experiences), how do you view each of the three emotions we're exploring: anger, guilt, and fear? How do you deal with each of these emotions?

_____

_____

_____

_____

3. **Your emotions do not have to dictate the direction of your life, including your struggle with depression.** It is possible to keep your emotions in balance so that they empower you and do not encumber you. But how can you know the difference between healthy anger, guilt, and fear and the versions that have turned destructive? The answer lies in the word _empowerment_. If your anger leaves you feeling determined to make some positive change in your life . . . and if guilt has opened your eyes to some area in your life that needs improvement . . . and if fear has alerted you to danger and motivated you to get out of harm's way, then your emotions have empowered you to be stronger, better, and wiser.

Your response: In what ways have anger, guilt, and fear been positive forces in your life? What changes have they inspired? How can you utilize these strong emotions in your quest to overcome depression?

_____

_____

_____

_____

Taking Stock

The most effective tool against runaway anger is awareness. Use the following questions to see your anger more clearly—and find ways to calm it.

It makes me angry when . . .

    1.

    2.

    3.

    4.

When I am on the verge of losing control of my anger, I feel (include physical sensations and emotions) . . .

    1.

    2.

    3.

    4.

Once my anger is triggered, I no longer feel able to . . .

    1.

    2.

3.

4.

When I'm angry, what I really want to say to people is . . .

1.

2.

3.

4.

Four strategies I know will help diffuse my anger, if I choose to
employ them, are . . .

1.

2.

3.

4.

If I could go back in time, what I would say to someone who
hurt me is . . .

1.

2.

3.

4.

What I will lose if I let go of my anger is . . .

1.

2.

3.

4.

What I will gain if I let go of my anger is . . .

1.

2.

3.

4.

Four healthy ways to express myself without anger are . . .

1.

2.

3.

4.

When I succeed in communicating without anger, I feel
(include physical sensations and emotions) . . .

1.

2.

3.

4.

Change Your Story, Change Your Life

1. What is the story you tell yourself about the three deadly emotions—anger, guilt, and fear? How were you raised to handle these strong feelings (e.g., suppress them, express them, deny them)? Describe some experiences when your emotions caused you trouble and other times when they helped you. Write out your story—just let it flow without self-editing or filtering.

----

2. Now write out a different narrative you want to embrace. Where do you want to end up? Describe your ideal life, free of destructive anger, guilt, and fear.

Dig Deeper

1. Which of the three deadly emotions—anger, guilt, and fear— has been most prevalent in your life? How so?

----

2. How has anger been a force in your life? Describe a time when anger served as a positive emotion for you (perhaps empowering you to stand up for yourself or to confront an injustice). Next, describe a time when your anger was counterproductive (perhaps causing a relationship rift that was not justified).

    _____

    _____

    _____

    _____

    _____

3. How has guilt been a force in your life? Describe a time when guilt served as a positive emotion for you (perhaps motivating you to correct a harmful behavior or repair a relationship). Next, describe a time when your guilt was counterproductive (such as feeling false guilt or apologizing for things you really didn't need to).

    _____

    _____

    _____

    _____

    _____

4. How has fear been a force in your life? Describe a time when fear served as a positive emotion for you (perhaps prompting you to protect yourself in a threatening situation or motivating you to prepare for a challenging situation). Next, describe a time when your fear was counterproductive (maybe resisting getting close to someone because of

painful past experiences or lashing out at someone for a
minor mistake).

_____

_____

_____

_____

5. As you consider the causes of your depression, to what degree
    do you think anger, guilt, and fear are contributing factors?
    In what ways do you want to work through these emotions so
    they don't bring you down?

_____

_____

_____

_____

First Steps, Next Steps

Now it's time to get practical. We've explored many issues that
prompted you to ponder and process. Let's put those thoughts into
action. I'll provide several steps forward, and then it's your turn to
determine three additional steps you will take this week.

1. Consider healthy ways to process your emotions—and act on
    your intentions. This might mean pursuing therapy with a
    qualified counselor, meeting regularly with a trusted friend,
    or joining a support group. Describe your plans.

_____

_____

_____

_____

2. Revisit a time when anger, guilt, or fear created hardship in your life. Write about the experience—and create a new ending to the story.

_____

_____

_____

_____

_____

_____

3. Write a note to yourself, describing how you would ideally like to handle your anger, guilt, and fear.

_____

_____

_____

_____

_____

_____

4. Your turn. What steps do you intend to take this week to move toward wellness?

a. _____

_____

_____

b. _____

_____

_____

c. _____

_____

_____

Closing Reflections

For people struggling with depression, the path to healing can seem long and laborious. Therefore, perseverance and stamina are essential. Because anger, guilt, and fear drain us and make our life seem dark, exhausting, and fraught with problems, it is vital for us to remember that while we are on the path to healing, our mind shows us the way, our spirit energizes us, and our body gets us there.

It's true that the pain of this world can erode our sense of joy and optimism. But God is able to take our negatives and turn them into positives. As you consider ways to fill yourself up with life-giving thoughts—an effective way to tame toxic emotions—start with these inspiring words from the apostle Paul:

> Rejoice in the Lord always. I will say it again: Rejoice! Let
> your gentleness be evident to all. The Lord is near. Do
> not be anxious about anything, but in every situation,
> by prayer and petition, with thanksgiving, present your
> requests to God. And the peace of God, which transcends
> all understanding, will guard your hearts and your minds
> in Christ Jesus. Finally, brothers and sisters, whatever
> is true, whatever is noble, whatever is right, whatever
> is pure, whatever is lovely, whatever is admirable—if
> anything is excellent or praiseworthy—think about
> such things.
> PHILIPPIANS 4:4-8

Negative emotions sap us of our mental and physical strength, but the opposite is also true: positive emotions invigorate us, giving us the boost we need to continue on through difficult stretches. This week, be intentional about identifying the thoughts that are dragging you down and replacing them with thoughts that lift you up.

Scripture for Meditation

Do not fear, for I am with you;
> do not be dismayed, for I am your God.

I will strengthen you and help you;
> I will uphold you with my righteous right hand.

ISAIAH 41:10

Wise Words to Awaken Your Spirit

The greatest discovery of my generation is that a human being can alter his life by altering his attitudes of mind.

WILLIAM JAMES

Journal Your Journey

This week you are going to be trying out new things, taking steps forward, forging new habits, and letting go of old ones. Will these things make a difference? Will you be able to discern any changes in how you feel and what you think?

This page is here for you to journal about the journey. What works? What doesn't? You'll know what to keep doing because you'll have your adventure documented in the pages of this workbook. Use this space to ask questions, make lists, doodle, write about your progress, and record milestones.

Let the adventure begin!

The Antidote for Toxic Emotions

*Forgiveness Is the Remedy—
and a Relief for Depression*

Chapter 7 at a Glance

Having learned that toxic emotions—anger, guilt, and fear—are serious obstacles on the road to lasting freedom from depression, it's easy to wonder, *What next? What can be done to deal with such formidable opponents?*

Thankfully, there is a proven antidote to toxic emotions—and a powerful tonic for regaining control over your health and well-being. However, like everything else on the road to healing depression for good, it's not a magic elixir you can ingest for instantaneous and miraculous relief. This cure will require tough choices, discipline, and commitment on your part. It will take courage to face the emotional dragons you've hidden away in your closet over the years and to dare to think differently about them. But it can be done! Proof lies in the millions of people who have gone before you and found freedom in the age-old practice of *forgiveness*.

I acknowledge that *forgiveness* is a loaded word for many people. It carries conflicting religious overtones or hints of pop culture sentimentalism many of us have learned to mistrust. For many of us, anger, guilt, fear, and judgment are more than mere emotions; they've become an armored identity. We wonder who and what we'll be if we let go.

And yet the reward for learning to let go is immense, particularly if you've been living under the shadow of depression.

Essential Ideas . . . and Your Insights

1. **The one who benefits most from forgiveness is you.** The purpose of forgiveness is not to deliver anything to the one who caused us harm but to help *ourselves* by letting go of toxic attachment to the past and to our pain. So long as we hang on to feelings of outrage, injustice, and desire for payback, we keep the offense alive and the wounds fresh. And in the process, we remain vulnerable to all the negative physical and psychological effects of runaway anger and fear.

    Your response: Have you experienced this truth in your own life? Specifically, have you resisted the challenge to forgive someone? If so, what repercussions and detriments did you encounter by choosing not to let go of an offense?

    _____

    _____

    _____

    _____

    _____

2. **Forgiveness is not about letting someone "off the hook."** When considering forgiveness, the most powerful objection we encounter in ourselves is the mistaken idea that to forgive

means looking the other way while somebody "gets away" with something. We see forgiveness as an undeserved get-out-of-jail-free card. That seems wrong somehow because we can't stand the idea of saying, "That's okay" about behavior that clearly is not.

Your response: Is this an issue for you—feeling like forgiveness is akin to shrugging off someone's bad behavior? What, for you, is involved in the process of acknowledging a person's hurtful acts yet fully forgiving that person?

_____

_____

_____

_____

3. **Forgiveness (or lack of it) gains momentum, bringing you more and more good health (or poor health).** If you choose not to forgive, you poison yourself, add more toxic shame to your life, and increase the desire to escape into unhealthy behaviors. But the good news is that forgiveness is like a snowball rolling downhill: once moving, it keeps growing and picking up speed. With the struggling clients I work with, I've seen time and time again that forgiveness helps lighten their emotional load, brighten their outlook on life, shorten their recovery time, and restore their natural resilience against the recurrence of depression in the future.

Your response: What other benefits come with the act of forgiveness? Specifically, how have _you_ benefited—emotionally, spiritually, physically—when you found the courage to forgive someone?

_____

_____

_____

_____

Taking Stock

Forgiveness is a practical and necessary step in healing from depression. Holding on to past hurts only deepens your feelings of anger, guilt, and fear. Use these questions to understand your resistance to forgiveness and how to overcome it.

I want to be able to forgive _____

for _____.

But I haven't yet let go of how that hurt me in these ways:

1.

2.

3.

4.

I'm afraid if I do forgive, it will mean . . .

1.

2.

3.

4.

I hope that forgiving this person will benefit me in the following ways:

1.

2.

3.

4.

Things I have learned about forgiveness that surprise me:

1.

2.

3.

4.

What forgiveness is to me:

1.

2.

3.

4.

What forgiveness isn't:

1.

2.

3.

4.

Things I need to ask someone else's forgiveness for:

1.

2.

3.

4.

Things I know I hold against God or life:

1.

2.

3.

4.

Strategies I know will help me let go of past hurts, if I choose to
employ them:

1.

2.

3.

4.

Change Your Story, Change Your Life

1. What is the story you tell yourself about forgiveness? What
    were the messages or role modeling you received in childhood
    about the issue of forgiveness? How have your spiritual beliefs
    and the teachings you received shaped your current willingness
    or unwillingness to forgive others (or yourself)? Write out your
    story—just let it flow without self-editing or filtering.

    _____

    _____

    _____

    _____

    _____

2. Now write out a different narrative you want to embrace.
    Where do you want to end up? Describe your ideal life,
    free of resentment.

    _____

    _____

    _____

    _____

    _____

Dig Deeper

1. What is your gut reaction when you hear the word *forgiveness*? To put it more personally, how do you feel when you hear the words (from yourself or someone else), "You really should forgive that person"?

   _____

   _____

   _____

   _____

   _____

2. What reasons do you give yourself for not forgiving someone who caused you harm? How can you work through these reasons?

   _____

   _____

   _____

   _____

3. Think of some instances when you needed to ask for someone's forgiveness for a mistake you made or hurt you caused. What were those experiences like for you? How did it feel when you received forgiveness—or when it was withheld?

   _____

   _____

   _____

   _____

4. Describe how your spiritual beliefs guide your thinking and actions about forgiveness. Do you find it difficult to live out the standards of forgiveness presented in Scripture? If so, in what way would you like to grow in this area?

_____

_____

_____

_____

_____

5. Do you feel the need to forgive God for anything? Some people take offense at the very idea that God, the Creator of all, would need to be forgiven. Yet it's a fact that many individuals feel angry at God or disappointed with him for allowing traumas or hardships to come into their lives (sometimes including depression). How do you react to this issue?

_____

_____

_____

_____

_____

First Steps, Next Steps

Now it's time to get practical. We've explored many issues that prompted you to ponder and process. Let's put those thoughts into action. I'll provide several steps forward, and then it's your turn to determine three additional steps you will take this week.

1. Take time to review your personal history—from years ago to recent times. Can you think of someone (or several people)

you need to forgive? Write about any resistance you feel about offering forgiveness. Next, create a plan to follow through on your intention to forgive.

_____

_____

_____

_____

_____

2. Review the misconceptions about forgiveness discussed in chapter 7 of *Healing Depression for Life*. Which of these misconceptions have you believed in the past? Identify other misconceptions you would add.

_____

_____

_____

_____

_____

3. Rewrite in your own words this passage from the apostle Paul: "Get rid of all bitterness, rage, anger, harsh words, and slander, as well as all types of evil behavior. Instead, be kind to each other, tenderhearted, forgiving one another, just as God through Christ has forgiven you" (Ephesians 4:31-32, NLT). Reflect on how you can put this Scripture into action in your life.

_____

_____

_____

_____

_____

4. Your turn. What steps do you intend to take this week to move toward wellness?

a. _____

_____

_____

b. _____

_____

_____

c. _____

_____

_____

Closing Reflections

If I were to distill the essence of this week's theme into an equation, it would be this: Forgiveness = Freedom. Forgiveness is the place where you experience release and relief from your own hurtful actions and the hurtful actions of others. Without that freedom, you will continue to carry toxic emotions that contaminate your heart and corrupt your thoughts.

Scripture tells us not to stay angry or hold grudges. Why? One reason is that anger is mostly harmful to the person who is angry. Unaddressed and unreleased anger is poisonous to the body, mind, and spirit.

So why don't we let it go? Because, ironically, it feels good to be mad. Anger amps up our adrenaline and energizes our emotions. What's more, it's simply *easier* to nurture anger than offer forgiveness. Author Frederick Buechner says,

> Of the seven deadly sins, anger is possibly the most fun. To lick your wounds, to smack your lips over grievances long past, to roll over your tongue the prospect of bitter confrontations still to come, to savor to the last toothsome morsel both the

pain you are given and the pain you are giving back—in many ways it is a feast fit for a king. The chief drawback is that what you are wolfing down is yourself. The skeleton at the feast is you.[10]

Such vivid imagery conveys the power of holding grudges and the need to work through the difficult process of letting them go. Personal transformation is attainable and healing depression is achievable . . . but both depend on a willingness to forgive.

Scripture for Meditation

As God's chosen people, holy and dearly loved, clothe yourselves with compassion, kindness, humility, gentleness and patience. Bear with each other and forgive one another if any of you has a grievance against someone. Forgive as the Lord forgave you. And over all these virtues put on love, which binds them all together in perfect unity.

COLOSSIANS 3:12-14

Wise Words to Awaken Your Spirit

Forgiveness is the key which unlocks the door of resentment and the handcuffs of hatred. It breaks the chains of bitterness and the shackles of selfishness.

CORRIE TEN BOOM

Journal Your Journey

This week you are going to be trying out new things, taking steps forward, forging new habits, and letting go of old ones. Will these things make a difference? Will you be able to discern any changes in how you feel and what you think?

This page is here for you to journal about the journey. What works? What doesn't? You'll know what to keep doing because you'll have your adventure documented in the pages of this workbook. Use this space to ask questions, make lists, doodle, write about your progress, and record milestones.

Let the adventure begin!

Strength through Soul Care

Spiritual Practices Are Essential to Healing from Depression

Chapter 8 at a Glance

Every page of *Healing Depression for Life* is built on the driving philosophy of treatment we have developed over the years at The Center: A Place of Hope—that wellness is a whole-person project. You've seen again and again that to be free, you must pay attention to *all* the sources of distress in your life. Leaving one problem area unexamined or one potential solution untried threatens to undermine all the work you've invested in everything else.

That's why I've included this chapter on an easily overlooked and undervalued dimension of your journey to lasting freedom—*faith*. Spiritual nutrition and healthy habits matter just as much as physical factors in your long-term recovery.

Now, in times of crisis, when well-meaning people advise you to "have faith," they often make it sound simple, as if it's possible to magically manufacture something as elusive as faith on command.

That's nearly as unhelpful as telling someone who's suffering from depression to simply "feel better." In previous chapters, you've learned that every step on the path to recovery requires courage and commitment on your part—all summed up in one powerful word: *choice.*

Faith is no different. It's not something ethereal we try to grasp; it's an action we take, on purpose, by choosing to believe we are not alone when the night is at its darkest. God does not need our faith; we do. His strength does not wane; ours does. Faith—precisely because it begins with a determined choice—is a jolt of energy that activates our spiritual and emotional immune system as nothing else can.

Soul care is about building connection to assets you didn't even know you had. Things like . . .

- **Strength.** The truth is, many of the habits, choices, and even addictions you must face when setting out to heal are frightening enough to tempt you to give up. Lots of people do just that. But it's not necessary to face them by yourself or on your own steam.
- **Comfort.** Psalm 23 begins, "The Lord is my shepherd; I have all that I need" (NLT). At times when the road seems impossibly long, having a spiritual refuge can make all the difference.
- **Guidance.** How often have you felt paralyzed by a choice you didn't know how to make? Jesus said, "Everyone who asks, receives. Everyone who seeks, finds. And to everyone who knocks, the door will be opened" (Matthew 7:8, NLT).

Soul care through faith is not simply a program to follow; it's a new way of life. It has the effect of transforming you from the inside out, shining light on the old things that no longer serve you and pointing to new ways of being that will. When faith works hand in hand with everything else you've learned in this book, the result can be breathtaking.

Essential Ideas . . . and Your Insights

1. **Faith is a choice.** Having faith begins with the simple act of choosing to believe we are not alone, even during our darkest times. You don't need to wait until you "feel" full of faith; you can begin with a determined choice.

    Your response: What kind of journey have you experienced so far with God? How has your faith journey evolved over time? What emotional response do you have to the idea of choosing to believe in a loving, personal God?

    ----

2. **Faith unlocks the door to hope.** Hopelessness is one of the key symptoms of depression, but faith stimulates hope. If you make a determined choice to believe in a powerful, loving Creator who knows you and cares about you, the natural next step is to begin to believe that good things are waiting for you in your future.

    Your response: Is hopelessness a familiar feeling for you? What difference would it make if you could experience an awakening of hope? What areas of your life are in the greatest need of a good dose of hope? Do you agree with the idea that even a little bit of hope makes a difference?

    ----

3. **There are actions you can take to embrace, express, exercise, and grow your faith.** As mentioned, faith isn't something you

simply wait to experience. It's not an ethereal emotion that you have or don't have. Instead, there are specific actions you can take that will exercise and grow faith (and hope) in your spirit.

Your response: Have you already made time in your week to pursue spiritual growth? If so, what does that look like? Are you surprised by the idea that faith is something you first choose and then act upon? Are you surprised that when it comes to faith, emotions don't play as big of a role as many people think they do?

Taking Stock

WHAT KIND OF "FAITH ACTIONS" ARE YOU CURRENTLY TAKING?

Place a check mark beside any of the actions you do at least once a week. If you do something at least weekly that is faith related and is not on the list, feel free to add it at the bottom:

- O Talk to God
- O Listen for his responses
- O Practice gratitude
- O Read the Bible or a devotional book
- O Come clean about your mistakes
- O Spend time with like-minded people who share your faith
- O Serve others
- O Cultivate a joyful heart
- O _____
- O _____

If you are not taking three or more actions every week to practice your faith, you are missing out on an opportunity to heal.

Change Your Story, Change Your Life

1. What is the story you tell yourself about your relationship with faith and God? Has your story evolved over the years? What experiences in your life have helped shape or even define the level of faith you are willing to commit to? Write out your story—just let it flow without self-editing or filtering.

_____

_____

_____

_____

_____

_____

_____

2. Now write out a different narrative you want to embrace. What do you wish you could believe? How might increased faith (and hope!) make a difference in your life?

_____

_____

_____

_____

_____

_____

Dig Deeper

1. What do you think of the idea that faith is an antidote to the hopelessness experienced by so many people with depression?

_____

_____

_____

_____

_____

_____

2. If you have made an intentional choice to have faith, describe what you have faith in. Or if you have not done so, describe the God in whom you would put your faith.

_____

_____

_____

_____

_____

_____

3. Have you asked God to help you choose to believe? If you have, what happened? If not, why not?

_____

_____

_____

_____

_____

_____

4. Do you know other people whose faith in God has been a positive experience for them and those around them? Write the names of these people below.

    _____

    _____

    _____

    _____

5. If you could tell God anything, what would you tell him? Write it below.

    _____

    _____

    _____

    _____

First Steps, Next Steps

Now it's time to get practical. We've explored many issues that prompted you to ponder and process. Let's put those thoughts into action. I'll provide several steps forward, and then it's your turn to determine three additional actions you will take this week.

1. Talk to God. Tell him about the things that are concerning you. Thank him for the good things in your life. Ask him for help in battling feelings of depression. Ask him to increase your faith.

    _____

    _____

    _____

    _____

2. Remember the list of people whose faith in God has been a positive experience for them and those around them (question 4 in "Dig Deeper")? Reach out to one of these people. Tell that person you are exploring ways to increase your faith, and see how the conversation develops from there.

    _____

    _____

    _____

    _____

    _____

3. This week, make a difference in the lives of others. Find someplace you can serve or otherwise reach out to people who would be thrilled to experience a helping hand from you.

    _____

    _____

    _____

    _____

    _____

4. Your turn. What steps do you intend to take this week to move toward wellness?

    a. _____

        _____

    b. _____

        _____

c. _____

_____

_____

Closing Reflections

There is a powerful verse in the book of Proverbs: "Hope deferred makes the heart sick" (13:12). And how true this is! When hope is lost and despair descends, the impact can be devastating and even terminal. And yet with hope, people not only discover new resiliency, but they can also find themselves surviving and even thriving once again.

If you have not considered yourself a person of faith to date, now may be the moment to change that. I know from my own experiences that faith and a relationship with God have been the life preserver I've hung on to in some of the roughest seas of life.

We can place our hope in a lot of things—our own smartness, guidance from others, degrees, money, plans, even people we love. And yet when these things fail—and at some point they will—it's good to have chosen to believe in a God who really does, like the old song says, have the whole world in his hands.

Scripture for Meditation

Why, my soul, are you downcast?
    Why so disturbed within me?
Put your hope in God,
    for I will yet praise him,
    my Savior and my God.

PSALM 42:11

Wise Words to Awaken Your Spirit

You never know how much you really believe anything until its truth or falsehood becomes a matter of life and death to you.

C. S. LEWIS

Journal Your Journey

This week you are going to be trying out new things, taking steps forward, forging new habits, and letting go of old ones. Will these things make a difference? Will you be able to discern any changes in how you feel and what you think?

This page is here for you to journal about the journey. What works? What doesn't? You'll know what to keep doing because you'll have your adventure documented in the pages of this workbook. Use this space to ask questions, make lists, doodle, write about your progress, and record milestones.

Let the adventure begin!

_____

_____

_____

_____

_____

_____

_____

_____

_____

_____

_____

_____

_____

_____

_____

_____

_____

_____

_____

_____

_____

_____

_____

Start Moving and Start Improving

Physical Activity Provides a Massive Boost to Your Mood and Metabolism

Chapter 9 at a Glance

This isn't a brand-new revelation. It's not rocket science either. Undoubtedly you've heard for years that exercise is good for your mood, body, and brain. Let's take a look at why this is the case.

With regard to mood and depression, exercise increases the release of critical chemicals and hormones that have a major impact on brain health and mood. These include norepinephrine, which improves focus and memory; dopamine, which gives you feelings of joy and accomplishment; serotonin, which regulates appetite, sleep, memory, sexual desire, and social behavior; and endorphins, which are linked to feelings of euphoria and well-being.

Exercise provides benefits to your physical health as well. Cardiovascular health is improved, bones and muscles are strengthened, and you will likely sleep better at night too.

What's more, exercise has an impact on attitude, improving confidence, boosting creativity, and giving you a healthy way to cope with the stresses of life.

And here's the really good news: it doesn't take hours of exercise a day to get these results. In fact, studies show that a majority of the benefits of exercise can be yours for the investment of about an hour a week.[11]

If you knew some—or all—of this, what's holding you back? Are you getting the amount of exercise you need for a healthier brain, body, and attitude?

Some people shy away from exercise, for any number of reasons. Perhaps they associate it with junior high gym class (not pretty for any of us!). They might associate exercise with repeated failures to lose weight. They might envision runners pounding the pavement, red faced and sweating profusely. And of course, depressed people often have little energy or motivation for physical activity.

My approach is simple: get moving. Do something—anything—and you will soon notice a change in your mood.

Essential Ideas . . . and Your Insights

1. **Exercise improves depression.** Studies show that exercise improves mood and has a positive impact on depression. John Ratey, MD, explains why in his book *Spark: The Revolutionary New Science of Exercise and the Brain.* According to Ratey, the depressed brain becomes locked in a negative loop. Exercise, he says, is the perfect tool for rebooting and reprogramming the stuck brain.[12]

    Your response: If you have experienced depression, have you ever felt that your brain was stuck in a negative loop? During seasons when you have felt most depressed, were you exercising? When you do exercise, what kind of differences can you detect in your body and mood?

_____

_____

_____

_____

2. **An hour a week is the magic number.** If you believe you don't have time to exercise enough to experience a real difference, think again. Studies show that when it comes to protecting people from depression, most of the benefits are realized with one hour of low-level exercise a week.

    Your response: If you are not exercising an hour a week, why not? Do you realize that an hour of exercise a week averages out to less than nine minutes a day? If an investment of nine minutes a day can make a significant difference in your health and mood, what's stopping you?

    _____

    _____

    _____

    _____

3. **Exercise is good for the rest of you too.** There is no part of your brain or body that is not positively impacted by exercise. In fact, Dr. Michael Bracko, chairman of the American College of Sports Medicine's Consumer Information Committee, says that "exercise is the magic pill," adding that it can literally cure some forms of heart disease, as well as cancer, arthritis, and depression.[13] It also strengthens bones and muscles and lowers blood sugar.

    Your response: In addition to depression, what other health issues do you struggle with? How might exercise play a role in improving these health issues?

_____

_____

_____

_____

Taking Stock

HOW FIT ARE YOU?

Take this quiz and find out. On a scale of 0 to 10, with 0 being very unlikely and 10 being very likely, how likely are you to . . .

- take the stairs instead of an elevator? _____
- do twenty minutes of aerobic exercise at least three times a week? _____
- park farther in the parking lot from your destination to increase your walk? _____
- do strength training (e.g., weight lifting) at least three times a week? _____
- find yourself standing and moving a lot during work hours? _____
- go to the gym this week? _____
- engage in a sport? _____

SCORING:

50 to 70—Congratulations! You are living an active lifestyle.

30 to 50—There is room for improvement, but you are definitely making an intentional effort to stay active.

0 to 30—What are you waiting for? Remember, you can experience many of the benefits of exercise by moving just ten minutes a day.

Change Your Story, Change Your Life

1. What is the story you tell yourself about your relationship with exercise? Has your story evolved over the years? What experiences in your life have helped shape or even define the level of movement you are willing to commit to? Write out your story—just let it flow without self-editing or filtering.

    ----

2. Now write out a different narrative you want to embrace. What do you wish you could believe? How might moving more make a difference in your life?

Dig Deeper

1. What negative experiences do you associate with exercise? (For example, getting picked last for sports teams as a child would qualify if it's the reason you now associate exercise with embarrassment and the feeling that you're not good enough.) How might these past experiences be influencing your activity level today?

    _____

    _____

    _____

    _____

2. Are there any sports or activities you've always wanted to tackle? For example, have you always wanted to climb a mountain? Scuba dive? Hike the Appalachian Trail? Learn to ski? What's keeping you from pursuing these things?

    _____

    _____

    _____

    _____

3. Proverbs 31 lists the traits of a woman of responsibility and influence in her family and community. In verse 17 we read that such a woman "sets about her work vigorously; her arms are strong for her tasks." How might exercise help you achieve and maintain strength for the kind of life you want to live?

    _____

    _____

    _____

    _____

4. What kinds of benefits would you experience if exercise were a regular part of your life (or if you already exercise, if you expanded your active lifestyle)?

----

5. Write down three lies you tell yourself about exercise. Now answer those lies with three corresponding truths.

First Steps, Next Steps

Now it's time to get practical. We've explored many issues that prompted you to ponder and process. Let's put those thoughts into action. I'll provide several steps forward, and then it's your turn to determine three additional actions you will take this week.

1. Start by making some sort of preparation this evening for moving more tomorrow. This might mean setting out workout clothes, rearranging your schedule to make time for a walk, or looking up the phone number of a local gym. Preparing today for an action you want to take tomorrow will help establish your commitment to actually taking that action tomorrow.

----

2. Identify a friend with whom you can go to the gym or just
    walk around the block. Having someone to exercise with can
    make the experience even more valuable—and it's harder to
    renege on your commitment to get moving when someone
    else is involved.

    _____

    _____

    _____

    _____

    _____

3. Make yourself a chart or calendar on which you can record
    how successful you are at incorporating more movement into
    your day, every day.

    _____

    _____

    _____

    _____

    _____

4. Your turn. What steps do you intend to take this week to move
    toward wellness?

    a. _____

       _____

       _____

    b. _____

       _____

       _____

c. _____

_____

_____

Closing Reflections

Life is such a gift. Taking care of our bodies helps us have the strength and stamina to make the most of this gift.

We also need strength and stamina to love and serve those around us, from our children and spouses and friends, to complete strangers who cross our paths. The point is, when we make the time to exercise, we are taking care of one of our greatest resources when it comes to enjoying life: our bodies.

You can do this. People of all ages, all walks of life, and all physical conditions have improved their mood and their lives by taking up exercise.

Scripture for Meditation

Don't you realize that in a race everyone runs, but only one person gets the prize? So run to win! All athletes are disciplined in their training. They do it to win a prize that will fade away, but we do it for an eternal prize. So I run with purpose in every step. I am not just shadowboxing. I discipline my body like an athlete, training it to do what it should. Otherwise, I fear that after preaching to others I myself might be disqualified.

1 CORINTHIANS 9:24-27, NLT

Wise Words to Awaken Your Spirit

Most of us think we don't have enough time to exercise. What a distorted paradigm! We don't have time not to. We're talking about three to six hours a week—or a minimum of thirty minutes a day, every other day. That hardly seems an inordinate amount of time considering the tremendous benefits in terms of the impact on the other 162–165 hours of the week.

STEPHEN COVEY

Journal Your Journey

This week you are going to be trying out new things, taking steps forward, forging new habits, and letting go of old ones. Will these things make a difference? Will you be able to discern any changes in how you feel and what you think?

This page is here for you to journal about the journey. What works? What doesn't? You'll know what to keep doing because you'll have your adventure documented in the pages of this workbook. Use this space to ask questions, make lists, doodle, write about your progress, and record milestones.

Let the adventure begin!

Good Food =
Good Mood

*Proper Nutrition and Hydration Fortifies
Your Body to Fend Off Depression*

Chapter 10 at a Glance

When it comes to understanding the need for a whole-person approach to treating depression, the content in this chapter is critical. After all, it addresses the fact that depression is not determined by just our brains and that tackling depression from all directions is imperative.

One of those directions happens to be from our stomachs.

What we eat determines whether or not our brains get essential nutrients. Our diets also determine the health of our microbiome, which is the collection of more than one hundred trillion bacteria that live in the gut.

When we eat nutrient-rich foods and have balanced, healthy guts, we are at less risk of depression. Likewise, if we eat junk food and have unbalanced, unhealthy guts, the odds of being depressed go up dramatically.[14]

Indeed, no serious intervention for depression can afford to overlook the power of food on mood. Altering the diet so the brain receives the nutrients it needs—and so the gut microbiome is healthy and balanced—may be one of the surest ways to experience relief from the bondage of depression.

Essential Ideas . . . and Your Insights

1. **Nutritious foods and supplements support mental health.**
   Studies show that a diet composed of fruits, vegetables, whole grains, fish, olive oil, and low-fat dairy is linked with a decreased risk of depression.[15] And in addition to the nutrients supplied by the food you eat, there are many supplements that are good for your brain and mood.

   Your response: When you think about what you are feeding your brain, what do you come up with? While it's important to stop feeding your brain junk food and chemicals, it's also important to make sure you are supporting your brain with the nutrition found in a healthy diet. Are brain-healthy foods (like those listed above) the foods you gravitate toward, or are they the foods you forget to eat or even avoid?

   _____

   _____

   _____

   _____

   _____

2. **The microbiome is a crucial component of mental health.** For people struggling with depression, gut health is critical, as there are strains of bacteria living in the gut that affect mood. The term that refers to this dynamic is *psychobiotics*, because some of these tiny organisms send messages to the brain that impact

anxiety, happiness, satisfaction, and depression. There are both beneficial and harmful bacteria in our guts, so maintaining the right balance is crucial. The good bacteria feed on plant-based fibers from whole foods. Guess what the bad bacteria feed on? Sugar. In fact, a diet high in sugar and processed foods is one of the greatest disrupters of a healthy microbiome.

Your response: Are you familiar with the idea that imbalances in the gut can impact depression? Based on your diet, which bacteria in your gut do you think are thriving—the good bacteria (which love plant-based fibers) or the bad bacteria (which love sugar)?

---

3. **A depressed brain is often deficient in key nutrients and neurotransmitters.** This is why fortifying and supporting your brain with supplemental vitamins and nutrients is critical.

Your response: Do you already take vitamins and supplements? What supplements have you taken in the past or are you currently taking? Do you know which supplements are particularly helpful for brain health? (Consider consulting chapter 13 in *Healing Depression for Life* for a list of helpful supplements.)

Taking Stock

IS YOUR BRAIN GETTING THE NUTRITION IT NEEDS?

The following foods and behaviors are good for your brain—and a healthy brain helps keep depression at bay. See what your brain needs, and decide whether your diet (food plus supplements) is supplying that need.

Your brain needs:	Here's where it comes from:	Is your diet giving your brain what it needs?	
Beta-carotene	apricots, broccoli, cantaloupes, carrots, collards, peaches, pumpkin, spinach, sweet potatoes	○ Yes	○ No
Vitamin C	blueberries, broccoli, grapefruits, kiwis, oranges, peppers, potatoes, strawberries, tomatoes	○ Yes	○ No
Vitamin D	salmon, egg yolk, yogurt, whole milk, almond milk, cheese	○ Yes	○ No
Selenium	beans and legumes, low-fat dairy, nuts and seeds, seafood, whole grains	○ Yes	○ No
Omega-3 fatty acids	fatty fish (mackerel, salmon, tuna), flaxseed, canola and soybean oils, walnuts, dark green leafy vegetables	○ Yes	○ No

Change Your Story, Change Your Life

1. What is the story you tell yourself about your relationship with healthy food and nutrition? Has your story evolved over the years? What do you know today about feeding your brain that

you didn't know ten years ago? Write out your story—just let it flow without self-editing or filtering.

_____

_____

_____

_____

_____

_____

_____

2. Now write out a different narrative you want to embrace. What do you wish you could believe? What habits do you want to adopt? How can eating less sugar and more whole foods make a difference in your life?

_____

_____

_____

_____

_____

_____

_____

Dig Deeper

1. We all have messages we tell ourselves about food and eating, so what are yours? They can be either positive or negative. These might include *I want to reward myself with something sweet . . . Healthy food is boring . . . I want to take care of myself*

by eating right . . . I'm too busy to cook—I'll just pick up fast food.
List some of your messages.

2. When you have tried to eat healthier in the past, what
   happened? How difficult was it to make different food choices?
   Did you feel like a success or a failure?

3. What foods are hardest for you to give up? Fast food? Processed
   snack foods? Sugar? Why are certain foods hard for you to
   bypass? Are there particular ideas you associate with these
   foods—for example, the idea of comfort, or even control (as in
   not wanting anyone to tell you what you can and cannot eat)?

4. Do you feel physically or psychologically addicted to certain foods, such as sugar? What is the longest you have gone without consuming any sugar at all?

_____

_____

_____

_____

_____

5. What immediate benefits do you feel when you avoid processed, sugary junk foods and eat whole foods instead? Talk about the impact on your emotions, energy, confidence, and ability to focus and remember.

_____

_____

_____

_____

_____

First Steps, Next Steps

Now it's time to get practical. We've explored many issues that prompted you to ponder and process. Let's put those thoughts into action. I'll provide several steps forward, and then it's your turn to determine three additional actions you will take this week.

1. Reduce or eliminate sugar in your diet. Evaluate your diet and lifestyle and decide the extent to which sugar in your diet needs to be addressed. Are you a sugar addict for whom a cold-turkey approach might be necessary? Do you already watch your sugar intake but see room for improvement? One tip: when reducing

your dependence on sugar, don't turn to sugar substitutes, which are sweeter than real sugar and make your brain and taste buds an even greater slave to the taste of sweet.

2. Go back to the chart of brain-healthy nutrients and related foods on page 109. If your diet is not supplying essential nutrients to your brain, fix that. Go to this week's grocery list and write down the brain-healthy foods you're going to purchase and incorporate into your diet this week.

3. Up your water intake. Your body is about 60 percent water and needs constant replenishing to stay hydrated. I tell my clients to drink the equivalent of half their body weight in ounces of water every day. Write down how you will make sure you get the water you need.

4. Your turn. What steps do you intend to take this week to move toward wellness?

   a. _____

   _____

   _____

   b. _____

   _____

   _____

   c. _____

   _____

   _____

Closing Reflections

In Genesis 1:29 God told the first humans, "Behold, I have given you every plant yielding seed that is on the face of all the earth, and every tree with seed in its fruit. You shall have them for food" (ESV).

We've come a long way from the Garden of Eden in terms of where we get our food. Perhaps you've seen the meme that says, "Thank God I don't have to hunt for food. I don't even know where tacos live." The point is, the typical American diet of man-made fake food brimming with sugar and chemicals is a far cry from how our bodies were designed to be fueled.

Isn't it time to get back to basics?

Scripture for Meditation

Do you not know that your bodies are temples of the Holy Spirit, who is in you, whom you have received from God? You are not your own; you were bought at a price. Therefore honor God with your bodies.

1 CORINTHIANS 6:19-20

Wise Words to Awaken Your Spirit

Different foods fuel different types of thoughts, different potentials for success, and different destinies or destinations in life. . . . Where are you headed with your current diet?

DAVID WOLFE, *EATING FOR BEAUTY*

Journal Your Journey

This week you are going to be trying out new things, taking steps forward, forging new habits, and letting go of old ones. Will these things make a difference? Will you be able to discern any changes in how you feel and what you think?

This page is here for you to journal about the journey. What works? What doesn't? You'll know what to keep doing because you'll have your adventure documented in the pages of this workbook. Use this space to ask questions, make lists, doodle, write about your progress, and record milestones.

Let the adventure begin!

Time to Take Out the Trash

Detox Your Body of Pollutants to Improve Your Overall Wellness

Chapter 11 at a Glance

It's easy to visualize the ravages of pollution in our environment. We see it in our own neighborhoods and cities. We see it in our skies. We've seen photos of it around the world. Clogged streams, littered beaches, steaming landfills, and billowing factory smokestacks are shocking visuals. No one believes for a moment that pollution doesn't exist or that it's not damaging our environment.

But when it comes to pollution in our bodies, we don't have the same visuals to help us understand the magnitude of the problem or the impact it has on the quality of our lives today and into the future.

The reality is that every day our bodies are exposed to toxic substances. We are exposed in our environments, by our food, and through our own choices to abuse drugs and other substances. Sometimes our bodies get "polluted" through inflammation caused by eating foods to which we are sensitive or allergic, such as gluten.

And while we don't have shocking photos of sea turtles tangled in plastic to drive home the idea that the pollution in our bodies is having a devastating impact, we feel that impact every day in the form of fatigue, cancer, anxiety, ADHD, depression, and more.

But we are not without hope—and strategies! The body has multiple organs and systems designed to work together to filter and flush out toxins. Sometimes these organs and systems become bogged down by the number of pollutants we are exposed to every day. Also, our lifestyles don't always support these organs and systems with the nutrients and activities they need to thrive.

But by being intentional about certain choices and behaviors, we can give our bodies what they need to filter incoming pollutants and even flush away the toxins that are already in our bodies and wreaking havoc in our lives.

Essential Ideas . . . and Your Insights

1. **There are chemicals and other substances in our environment—and especially in the food we eat—that contribute to depression.** In fact, these neurotoxins are also linked to brain tumors, Alzheimer's, migraines, chronic fatigue, ALS, insomnia, inflammation, brain fog, memory loss, thyroid dysfunction, and much more.

    Your response: If a toxin in your food or environment were dramatically increasing your risk of the diseases mentioned above, would you want to know about it? Do the toxins in your food and environment feel like less of a "real threat" because you can't see them? Explain.

    _____

    _____

    _____

    _____

2. **Consuming food and beverages is the most common way we get toxins into our bodies.** The standard Western diet consists mostly of high-sugar, highly processed, chemically enhanced substances brimming with neurotoxins.

    Your response: Are you willing to change your diet if it means relief from depression and other mental and physical concerns? What food or drink items would be most difficult for you to give up or replace?

    _____

    _____

    _____

    _____

3. **By detoxing, you are freeing your body to take better care of your health and your mood.** Detoxing is a great way to address many of the neurotoxins that come our way. When I see a new client struggling with depression, I often recommend a three-week protocol designed to cleanse and detox the body. It uses detox agents, changes in what you are eating, and actions that support your body's natural inclination to detox itself.

    Your response: Have you ever done a three-week cleanse before? What did you think about it? Did you find it helpful?

    _____

    _____

    _____

    _____

Taking Stock
IS FOOD THE CULPRIT?

On a scale of 0 to 10, with 0 being very unlikely and 10 being very likely, how likely are you to eat or drink the following in a given week?

- alcoholic beverages _____
- foods that contain additives and artificial preservatives, food colorings, artificial thickeners, and/or a variety of chemicals _____

- chemical sweeteners, including Nutrasweet, Equal, Spoonful, and any other artificial sweetener found in processed foods or drinks _____
- processed foods and snacks, including things made with refined carbohydrates, refined grains, and white flour _____
- fried foods _____
- fish from rivers or lakes with high levels of mercury _____
- fruits and vegetables grown with the use of pesticides and herbicides _____

SCORING:

50 to 70—Danger Zone. You need to change your diet immediately to avoid toxin-laden "foods."

30 to 50—There is room for improvement.

0 to 30—You are eating fairly clean. Keep up the good work!

Change Your Story, Change Your Life

1. What is the story you tell yourself about your relationship with high-sugar, high-fat foods? Or perhaps your relationship with alcohol, another neurotoxin? Much of our attitude about eating is shaped during our growing-up years—so how did your upbringing shape your perspective? Has your story evolved over the years? Write out your story—just let it flow without self-editing or filtering.

_____

_____

_____

_____

_____

_____

_____

2. Now write out a different narrative you want to embrace. What do you wish you could believe? How might detoxing from the toxic substances you ingest make a difference in your life?

_____

_____

_____

_____

_____

Dig Deeper

1. Food allergies or sensitivities can cause inflammation and reactions in the body that can be just as devastating as the damage caused by toxins. Celiac disease and gluten sensitivity are two of the more common ones. You probably know people who suffer from these sensitivities and have altered their diet as a result. Have you been diagnosed with either one of these conditions? If so, how successful have you been at altering your diet? If not, have you ever wondered if gluten could be contributing to your depression?

_____

_____

_____

_____

2. One study linked one alcoholic drink a day with an increased
    risk of brain damage. In fact, individuals who had a drink
    a day were *three times more likely* to have brain atrophy as a
    result.[16] How much alcohol do you consume on a regular basis?
    Knowing that alcohol is a neurotoxin that damages the brain
    and contributes to depression, how willing are you to change
    your consumption habits?

    _____

    _____

    _____

    _____

3. It takes discipline to change your diet to eliminate foods
    causing inflammation and those laden with chemicals. Is that a
    daunting idea? Have you had success with discipline/willpower
    with regard to food and drink in the past? If not, why not?
    Some foods have an addictive quality. Could this be keeping
    you from having willpower in this area? If so, what are your
    options?

    _____

    _____

    _____

    _____

4. Having a partner on the journey for accountability and
    encouragement can be a big help, especially when you are
    trying to change ingrained habits. Have you had success
    changing habits in the past by partnering with others on the

same journey? Can you identify someone who could fulfill this role when it comes to changing your eating or drinking habits or sticking with a three-week detox protocol?

_____

_____

_____

_____

_____

First Steps, Next Steps

Now it's time to get practical. We've explored many issues that prompted you to ponder and process. Let's put those thoughts into action. I'll provide several steps forward, and then it's your turn to determine three additional actions you will take this week.

1. On page 125, you'll find the three-week protocol I recommend for detoxing the body of pollutants that may be contributing to depression. Today, make preparations to begin following the protocol for three weeks, starting as soon as you're able. List your plans here.

_____

_____

_____

_____

_____

2. Many of the steps in the three-week protocol are actions you can incorporate into your life on an ongoing basis. Drinking water, getting a good night's sleep, and getting daily exercise, for example, should be part of your daily routine from now on.

Write some practical steps and goals for following the detox
protocol beyond the three-week detox period.

_____

_____

_____

_____

_____

_____

3. Make yourself a chart or calendar on which you can record how
   successful you are at avoiding toxin-laden food and drink.

_____

_____

_____

_____

_____

4. Your turn. What steps do you intend to take this week to move
   toward wellness?

   a. _____

   _____

   b. _____

   _____

   c. _____

   _____

Three-Week Detox Protocol

Detox Agents

Every day, do at least two of these:

- Drink a cup of dandelion root tea in the morning and again in the afternoon.
- Take 500 mg of N-acetyl cysteine (NAC) twice a day.
- Take 300 mg of milk thistle (extracted from the fruit or seed, not the leaf, and standardized to 70 to 80 percent of the active ingredient silymarin).

Dietary Changes

- Eliminate *all* alcohol, soda, energy drinks, coffee, and juices or teas with added sugar.
- Avoid all candy and other sweets.
- Drink two cups or more of fresh-pressed vegetable juice every day.
- Limit animal products. Eat no more than six ounces of animal flesh a day.
- Avoid all dairy products except for butter.
- Focus on whole foods (whatever you can buy in the produce section).
- Drink at least two liters of water a day.

Moving the Blood and Lymphatics

Every day, do at least two of the following:

- Dry skin brushing, which involves brushing your skin with a soft brush prior to a bath or shower. This provides gentle exfoliation, boosts circulation, and encourages new cell growth.

- Spend time in a sauna, then follow up with a cold rinse for ninety seconds or less. (I recommend choosing this at least three times a week.)
- Exercise for at least twenty to thirty minutes at a time. Exercise boosts circulation through the body, which helps flush toxins out.

Sleep

Get at least seven and a half hours of sleep a night. This will not only help you feel rested and less stressed but it will also reduce inflammation so your body can function at its best.

If you decide to follow the protocol for yourself, in addition to helping your body get rid of built-up toxins, this plan also eliminates foods—gluten, corn, soy, dairy, eggs, and sugar—that are common causes of food sensitivities and inflammation in the body. What this means is that, after following this protocol for three weeks, you are in the perfect position to slowly reintroduce common problem foods back into your diet, paying close attention to any reactions you may be having.

Pick one of the foods that was eliminated—bread, for example—and eat it twice a day for two days. Keep a journal (or use the journaling page at the end of this week in the workbook) and write down any differences you notice in your body, energy, or mood. Do you feel more depressed? Have headaches or joint pain? Feel bloated or fatigued? Are you experiencing brain fog or trouble concentrating?

If your body responds negatively to that food, remove it again from your diet. Wait a few days, then reintroduce a different food and pay attention to how your body responds.

Whether you have gluten sensitivities or not, when it comes to managing your mood, clean eating is going to make a major difference.

Closing Reflections

The saying goes that "ignorance is bliss." Likewise, denial can be fun—for a season. It's no secret that a diet filled with chemical-infused fake food, or overindulging with alcohol, is bad for your mood, brain, and body. In fact, the chemicals in our diets have been linked not only to depression but also to ADHD, cancer, and more.

Knowing what you know, how long are you going to put off taking action? With fast-food drive-thru restaurants on every corner and fake food calling our names from every grocery store aisle, nothing is going to change on its own. You will need to be intentional about changing what you put in your mouth. Take charge of your mood and your health by taking charge of what you eat. And don't wait. Denial is fun only for a season; eventually, years of poor choices will catch up with you, and your physical or mental health will suffer as a result.

Scripture for Meditation

Dear friend, I pray that you may enjoy good health and that all may go well with you, even as your soul is getting along well.

3 JOHN 1:2

Wise Words to Awaken Your Spirit

You need to put what you learn into practice and do it over and over again until it's a habit. I always say "Seeing is not believing. Doing is believing." There is a lot to learn about fitness, nutrition and emotions, but once you do, you can master them instead of them mastering you.

BRETT HOEBEL

Journal Your Journey

This week you are going to be trying out new things, taking steps forward, forging new habits, and letting go of old ones. Will these things make a difference? Will you be able to discern any changes in how you feel and what you think?

This page is here for you to journal about the journey. What works? What doesn't? You'll know what to keep doing because you'll have your adventure documented in the pages of this workbook. Use this space to ask questions, make lists, doodle, write about your progress, and record milestones.

Let the adventure begin!

Reinventing Your Future

Maintain Your Momentum for the Rest of Your Life

Chapter 14 at a Glance

If you've truly invested the will and the work necessary to take charge of healing depression for life, the moment has come for you to reap the full reward. It's time to think about the *future*.

Up until this point in your journey, you've focused on the past—by facing toxic emotions and thought patterns that have kept you trapped; by owning up to old mistakes and forgiving people who have failed you in some way; and by examining how your own choices have helped create your experience of life.

You've also thought a lot about the present. You've considered things like current addictions, sleep habits, diet, and unhelpful behavioral patterns that have dominated your daily life. Together, we've examined the various treatment options available to you today in your quest to be free of depression for good.

When you picked up this book and took your first steps on the road to recovery, the future probably felt like a black hole—no light, no hope of escape, no clear beginning or end. That's the nature of depression. Any attempt to see beyond present darkness becomes incredibly frightening. So you stop trying. But now that well-being is a reality for you again, and momentum is back on your side, it's time to take another look.

It's once again safe to think bigger and aim higher than you did when simply "getting by." That sounds good, but if you're like most people, you're wondering, *How?* This chapter answers that question with a series of practical steps you can take today into a better future tomorrow.

There is nothing more exciting than realizing that the rest of your life can be what you choose to make it. Yes, unforeseen challenges will always be part of the fabric of life. But those need not have the final say in how you experience the world. That power belongs to you.

Essential Ideas . . . and Your Insights

1. **Many people overcoming depression must renew and reboot their dreams for the future.** You haven't fought this hard and come this far just to plod through a mediocre life. An *extraordinary* future is now yours for the taking. You're free—not just from depression, but free to succeed, to grow, to have adventures, to meet new people, to learn new things, to experience new reasons to love life. In other words, you are just like everyone else—empowered to have your life the way you want it.

    Your response: Since you have been focused on the daily challenges of depression for months or even years, have you lost sight of what a fulfilling future looks like for you? How can you begin the process of renewing and reformulating your plans for the years ahead?

------

2. **Reactivate your imagination to draw inspiration about the future.** In the depths of depression, your imagination was hijacked and habituated to project only dull, dark, and dreary outcomes. That state of mind imagines worst-case scenarios. It projects hardship and lack everywhere it looks. And since seeing is the precursor to creating, is it any surprise that this is the vision the world reflected back to you? To build a brighter future, begin by imagining—in vivid detail—exactly what you want it to look like.

   Your response: Do you feel like depression dampened the playful, positive aspect of your imagination? How can you reenergize your ability to dream, brainstorm, and visualize your future?

------

3. **Envisioning a meaningful future involves reclaiming your life's purpose.** I define purpose as the *one unique thing* we each have to offer the world, no matter how big or small. Its absence might not make headlines, but it absolutely would be missed by those who stand to benefit from your gifts. Your personal purpose might center on raising healthy children, volunteering

with the elderly, sharing your musical talents with the world, preserving the earth's environment, or demonstrating the love of God through acts of service. The list of possibilities is infinite. Only you can know which one best describes you.

Your response: Do you currently have a clear sense of purpose in life? If not, did you at some point? What was it? Without trying to come up with the final answer right now, jot down some possible unique life-purpose ideas that inspire and energize you.

_____

_____

_____

_____

Taking Stock

A brighter future awaits anyone who stops letting past choices and disappointments write the script. The following questions will help you see the obstacles in your way—and see that you have the power to clear them and move on.

Things I loved to do when I was younger:

1.

2.

3.

4.

My reasons for stopping those things:

1.

2.

3.

4.

Things that would make me happy now if money/time/the
approval of others were no obstacle:

1.

2.

3.

4.

Possible reasons why I am alive on earth (hint: gifts and talents
you possess that the world needs):

1.

2.

3.

4.

Excuses I've made for not pursuing my dreams and purpose:

1.

2.

3.

4.

What I fear it would cost to boldly follow my dreams:

1.

2.

3.

4.

What I secretly hope I might gain:

1.

2.

   3.

   4.

Steps I can take today in the direction of my dreams:

   1.

   2.

   3.

   4.

Things I can do in the next year (or five, ten, or twenty years) to stop sitting on the sidelines of my life and get in the game:

   1.

   2.

   3.

   4.

My answers to anyone (including myself) who says I can't achieve all this and more:

   1.

   2.

   3.

   4.

Change Your Story, Change Your Life

1. What is the story you tell yourself about your dreams for the future and your purpose in life? Has your story evolved over the years? What experiences have influenced your thinking about your direction in life? How has depression changed your

perspective about your future? Write out your story—just let it flow without self-editing or filtering.

_____

_____

_____

_____

_____

_____

_____

_____

_____

_____

2. Now write out a different narrative you want to embrace. What do you wish you could believe? What habits do you want to adopt? What dreams and direction do you want to pursue?

_____

_____

_____

_____

_____

_____

_____

_____

_____

_____

Dig Deeper

1. How do you think depression has affected your outlook on your future? As you experience progress toward wellness, do you feel more enthusiastic about your life as you look ahead?

    ----

2. Many people believe that joy comes naturally and effortlessly into our lives. But often we must *choose* joy and intentionally find ways to experience it. So this week, how can you invite joy into your life? Write out several specific ideas.

    ----

3. In the "Essential Ideas" section of this week, I wrote, "You haven't fought this hard and come this far just to plod through a mediocre life. An *extraordinary* future is now yours for the taking. You're free—not just from depression, but free to succeed, to grow, to have adventures, to meet new people, to learn new things, to experience new reasons to love life." How do you feel when you read these words? Explain why you respond the way you do.

    ----

4. It's likely depression has stolen your desires from you—and it's time to take them back. Reclaiming your desires is really about remembering what you *love*. When you were a kid, nobody could stop you from doing what you loved, which might have been drawing, roller-skating, playing board games, or doing crafts. Write some of your favorite activities from childhood, and think about doing some of them again, all these years later. Recapturing a childlike spirit will make you a happier adult.

_____

_____

_____

_____

5. I pointed out in this chapter that everyone struggles and that these struggles eventually make us stronger if we'll allow them to. That means you need not look back on depression with regret but rather with hope since you've survived the ordeal in order to be stronger and better than ever. Record some of the ways the challenge of depression has taught you important lessons and made you a stronger person.

_____

_____

_____

_____

First Steps, Next Steps

Now it's time to get practical. We've explored many issues that prompted you to ponder and process. Let's put those thoughts into action. I'll provide several steps forward, and then it's your turn to determine three additional actions you will take this week.

1. It's remarkable how often people have trouble finishing
    the simple sentence, "I want . . ." Somehow, the process of
    growing up teaches most of us to think of what we want out
    of life as secondary to . . . well, just about everything and
    everyone else. But desire is the fuel that powers achievement.
    To test yourself for a lost connection to your desires, write in
    the space below several sentences that begin with "I want . . ."
    The only rule is you can't write something that's for someone
    else. Each item must reflect something you want for yourself.

    _____

    _____

    _____

    _____

    _____

2. Here's the secret to finding your purpose: start by looking
    again at the list you made of things you have loved in your
    life. Chances are, what you're meant to do now is something
    you couldn't stop doing as a younger person but that you
    abandoned along the way. Or it may be the thing you still
    didn't dare put on the list but that tugs at your sleeve anyway.
    Write down some things you felt passionate about in the past
    that might be revived now.

    _____

    _____

    _____

    _____

3. Find a friend who will join you in pursuing a new activity—an art class, a new hobby, or something else that is both fun and challenging. Name some people you can ask to join you and list possible activities you could do together.

4. Your turn. What steps do you intend to take this week to move toward wellness?

   a.

   b.

   c.

Closing Reflections

I've worked with hundreds of people who felt unfulfilled in their lives. They felt dissatisfied and disappointed. Though these men and women generally worked hard doing good things, they had a nagging sense that they were missing out on something.

Indeed, many people struggle with the questions "What am I really here for? What's my unique purpose and calling?" They want to do something meaningful and significant with their lives . . . but what? And of course, depression has a way of clouding our vision and diminishing our self-esteem, putting a sense of purpose further out of reach.

That's why prayer, reflection, and journaling can be so helpful. Creating the space in your life to explore, contemplate, and dream enables you to determine and define what exactly will be your remarkable contribution to the world. When you tune out all the voices around you screaming for attention, you can listen to your own inner voice and the voice of God. When you are vitally aware of what's going on within you and in your surroundings, your reason for living will become distinctly evident.

When you discover your unique God-given purpose, the excitement of life returns and depression recedes. You know that each day presents opportunities to fulfill your potential and move you in a positive direction. That is the joyful life God intends for you—one full of hope for the future.

Scripture for Meditation

May the God of hope fill you with all joy and peace as you trust in him, so that you may overflow with hope by the power of the Holy Spirit.

ROMANS 15:13

Wise Words to Awaken Your Spirit

Quit living as if the purpose of life is to arrive safely at death. Set God-sized goals. Pursue God-ordained passions. Go after a dream that is destined to fail without divine intervention. Keep asking questions. Keep making mistakes. Keep seeking God. Stop pointing out problems and become part of the solution. Stop repeating the past and start creating the future. Stop playing it safe and start taking risks. Expand your horizons. Accumulate experiences. Enjoy the journey. Find every excuse you can to celebrate everything you can. Live like today is the first day and last day of your life.

MARK BATTERSON

Journal Your Journey

This week you are going to be trying out new things, taking steps forward, forging new habits, and letting go of old ones. Will these things make a difference? Will you be able to discern any changes in how you feel and what you think?

This page is here for you to journal about the journey. What works? What doesn't? You'll know what to keep doing because you'll have your adventure documented in the pages of this workbook. Use this space to ask questions, make lists, doodle, write about your progress, and record milestones.

Let the adventure begin!

Notes

1. Amy Morin, "Depression Statistics Everyone Should Know," Verywell Mind, updated August 22, 2018, https://verywellmind.com/depression-statistics-everyone-should -know-4159056.
2. "Major Depression," National Institute of Mental Health, updated November 2017, https://www.nimh.nih.gov/health/statistics/major-depression.shtml.
3. A summary of research findings can be accessed at Seth J. Gillihan, "What Is the Best Way to Treat Depression?" *Psychology Today*, May 30, 2017, https://www.psychology today.com/us/blog/think-act-be/201705/what-is-the-best-way-treat-depression. Also see P. Cuijpers et al., "A Meta-analysis of Cognitive-Behavioural Therapy for Adult Depression, Alone and in Comparison with Other Treatments," *Canadian Journal of Psychiatry* 58, no. 7 (July 2013): 376–85. S. M. de Maat et al., "Relative Efficacy of Psychotherapy and Combined Therapy in the Treatment of Depression: A Meta-analysis," *European Psychiatry* 22, no. 1 (January 2007): 1–8.
4. Charles R. Swindoll, *Hope Again* (Nashville: Thomas Nelson, 1997), 277.
5. David Nutt, Sue Wilson, and Louise Paterson, "Sleep Disorders as Core Symptoms of Depression," *Dialogues in Clinical Neuroscience* 10, no. 3 (September 2008): 329–36, https://www.ncbi.nlm.nih.gov/pmc/articles/PMC3181883/.
6. "1 in 3 Adults Don't Get Enough Sleep," CDC Newsroom, CDC, last modified February 16, 2016, https://www.cdc.gov/media/releases/2016/p0215-enough-sleep .html. See also "Data and Statistics: Short Sleep Duration among US Adults," Sleep and Sleep Disorders, CDC, last modified May 2, 2017, https://www.cdc.gov/sleep /data_statistics.html.
7. Craig Groeschel, *Weird: Because Normal Isn't Working* (Grand Rapids, MI: Zondervan, 2011), 40.
8. George M. Slavich and Michael R. Irwin, "From Stress to Inflammation and Major Depressive Disorder: A Social Signal Transduction Theory of Depression,"

Psychological Bulletin 140, no. 3 (May 2014): 774–815, https://www.ncbi.nlm.nih
.gov/pmc/articles/PMC4006295/.

9. Therese J. Borchard, "Spirituality and Prayer Relieve Stress," Psych Central, updated
July 8, 2018, https://psychcentral.com/blog/spirituality-and-prayer-relieve-stress/.

10. Frederick Buechner, *Beyond Words: Daily Readings in the ABC's of Faith* (New York:
HarperCollins, 2004), 18.

11. Samuel B. Harvey et al., "Exercise and the Prevention of Depression: Results of the
HUNT Cohort Study," *American Journal of Psychiatry* 175, no. 1 (October 2017):
28–36, https://ajp.psychiatryonline.org/doi/abs/10.1176/appi.ajp.2017.16111223
?mobileUi=0&journalCode=ajp.

12. John J. Ratey with Eric Hagerman, *Spark: The Revolutionary New Science of Exercise
and the Brain* (New York: Little, Brown, 2008), 129, 136.

13. Michael Bracko, quoted at Dulce Zamora, "Fitness 101: The Absolute Beginner's
Guide to Exercise," WebMD, February 12, 2008, https://www.webmd.com/fitness
-exercise/features/fitness-beginners-guide#1.

14. Monique Tello, "Diet and Depression," *Harvard Health Blog*, February 22, 2018,
https://www.health.harvard.edu/blog/diet-and-depression-2018022213309.

15. Ye Li et al., "Dietary Patterns and Depression Risk: A Meta-analysis," *Psychiatry
Research* 253 (July 2017): 373–82, https://www.ncbi.nlm.nih.gov/pubmed
/28431261.

16. Melaina Juntti, "Just 5 Drinks a Week Can Damage Your Brain," *Men's Journal*,
accessed March 8, 2019, https://www.mensjournal.com/health-fitness/just-5-drinks
-a-week-can-damage-your-brain-w493425/.